AF022

MASSIMILIANO AFIERO

AXIS FORCES 22

WW2 AXIS FORCES

SOLDIERSHOP PUBLISHING

The Axis Forces 022 - First edition February 2023 by Luca Cristini Editor for the brand Soldiershop
Cover & Art Design by soldiershop factory.   ISBN code: 978-88-93279543
Copyright © 2023 Luca Cristini Editore (BG) ITALY.   No part of this publication may be reproduced, stored in a retrieval system or transmitted by any form or by any means, electronic, recording or otherwise without the prior permission in writing from the publishers. The publisher remains to disposition of the possible having right for all the doubtful sources images or not identifies. Visit www.soldiershop.com to read more about all our books and to buy them.

WW2 AXIS FORCES

The Axis Forces number 22 – February 2023

<u>Direction and editing:</u> Via San Giorgio, 11 – 80021 AFRAGOLA (NA) -ITALY
Managing and Chief Editor: Massimiliano Afiero
Email: maxafiero@libero.it - **Website**: www.maxafiero.it

Contributors

Tomasz Borowski, Grégory Bouysse, Stefano Canavassi, Carlos Caballero Jurado, Rene Chavez, Gary Costello, Paolo Crippa, Carlo Cucut, Antonio Guerra, John B. Köser, Lars Larsen, Christophe Leguérandais, Eduardo M. Gil Martínez, Michael D. Miller, Peter Mooney, Danilo Morisco, Péter Mujzer, Ken Niewiarowicz, Erik Norling, Raphael Riccio, Marc Rikmenspoel, Samcevich Andrei, Hugh Page Taylor, Charles Trang, Sergio Volpe

Editorial

Here at last is the new, first issue of 2023. Forgive us again for not having respected the publication times of our magazine, which with this very issue comes out in a new format with a greater number of pages. The main exigency is to be able to better deal with certain topics and to be able to publish them all at once, without having to split them up into several parts, considering that the magazine comes out every three months. Having more space available, we can finally include new research always giving space to the iconographic aspect, with new unpublished photos from the various war fronts. Naturally, in the next issues we will try to give more space to the foreign voluntary formations of the Wehrmacht *and the* Waffen-SS *and in general to all the other formations of the Axis. We therefore ask everyone of you for greater collaboration, above all in indicating and reporting to us topics of greater interest to be treated, always in the context of the Second World War. Let us now analyze the contents of this new issue of the magazine. We begin with a long and interesting work on the employment of the* Totenkopf *division during the counter-offensive on the Ukrainian front between February and March 1943, following the SS-Panzer-Korps. This is followed by the biography of* Egon Christophersen, *a Danish non-commissioned officer first in the* Wiking *division and then in the* Nordland *division, who distinguished himself during the fighting on the Narva front, earning himself the Knight's Cross. We continue with an article on the Tunisia campaign, fought by the Italian-German forces between the end of 1942 and the spring of 1943. We close with the second part of the article dedicated to the* Wiking *division in the Caucasian regions in the summer of 1942. Always hoping to have met your interest in military history, I wish you all a good read and see you in the next issue.*

Massimiliano Afiero

The publication of The Axis Forces deals exclusively with subjects of a historical military nature and is not intended to promote any type of political ideology either present or past, as it also does not seek to exalt any type of political regime of the past century or any form of racism.

Contents

Totenkopf on the Ukrainian Front, February-March 1943	Pag. 5
SS-Unterscharführer Egon Christophersen	Pag. 56
The Tunisian campaign	Pag. 63
The SS-Division Wiking towards the Caucasus, Summer 1942	Pag. 82

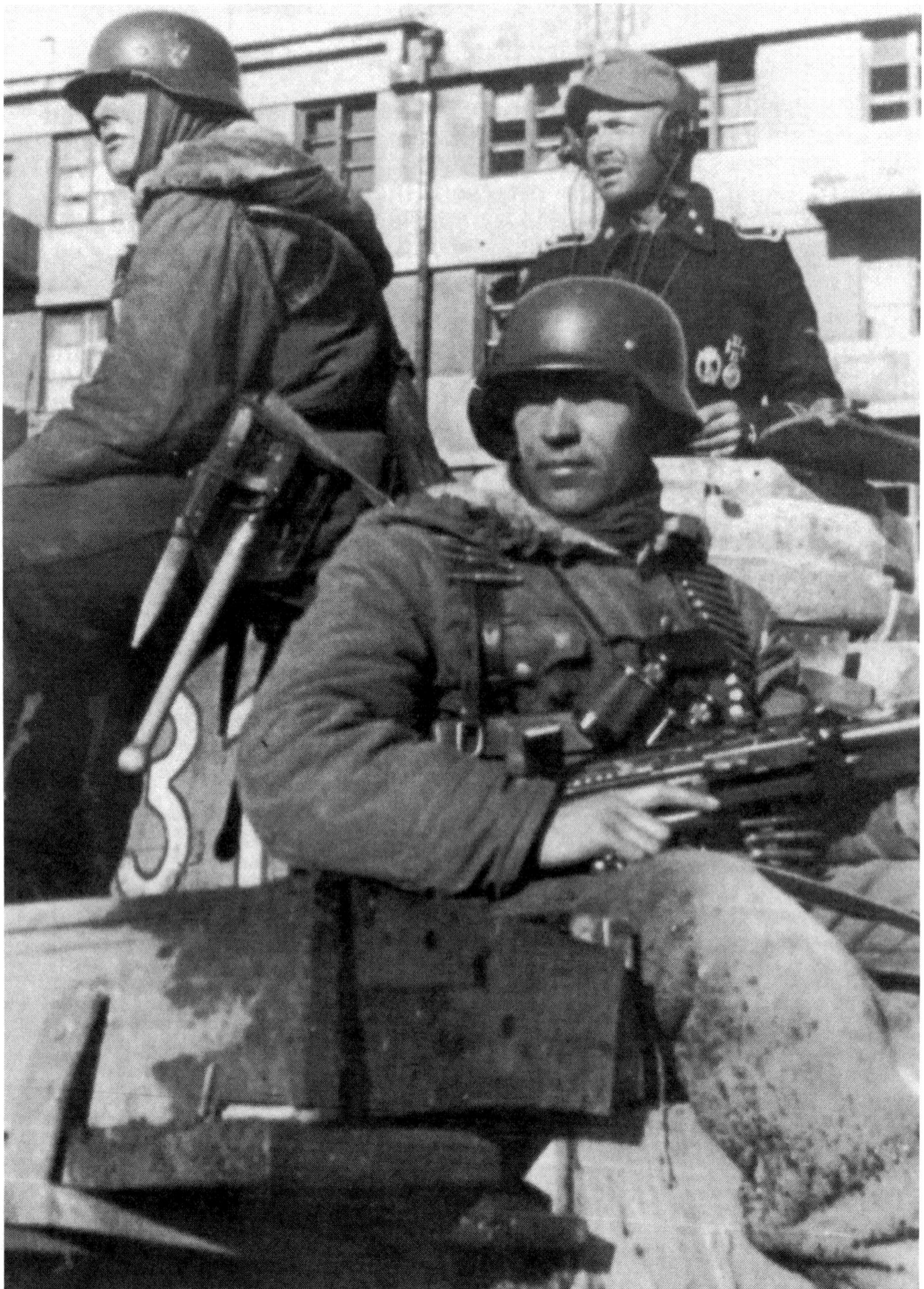

Totenkopf on the Ukrainian Front February-March 1943

by Massimiliano Afiero

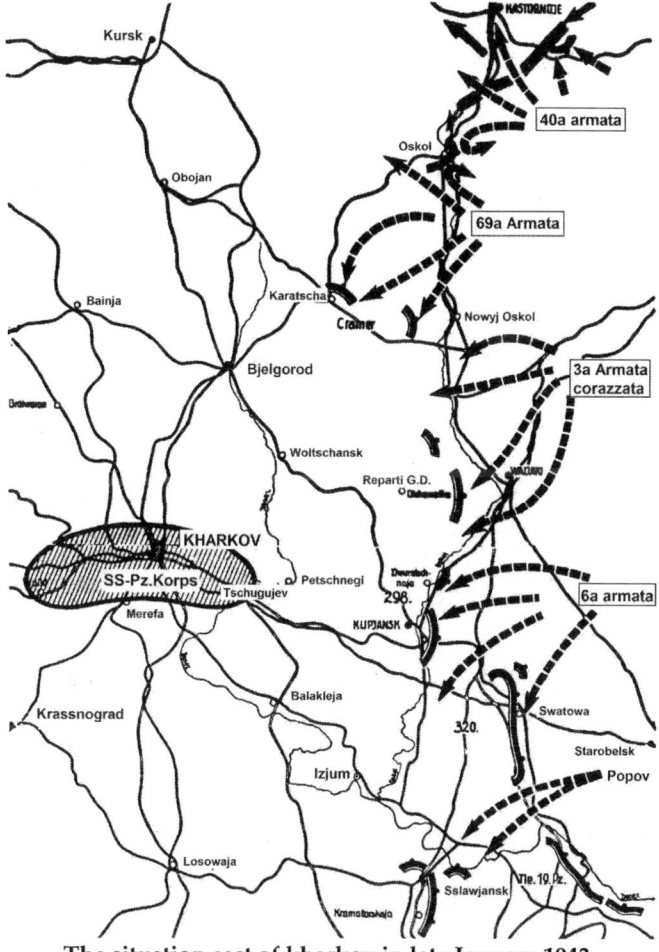

The situation east of kharkov in late January 1943.

Soviet infantry attacking the snowy steppe.

On January 31, 1943, the leading elements of *Totenkopf* left the Angoulême railway station and their convoys reached Kiev on February 7. From there, using their own vehicles, they were to move to their designagted areas. The division's new drivers were put quickly to the test on the icy and snowy roads, where trucks and vehicles slid continuously, causing accidents. In the meantime, the situation on the Ukrainian front had gotten worse; on February 3, 1943, Hitler personally ordered *SS-Ogruf.* Paul Hausser to move with his divisions from the area south of Kharkov towards Kupyansk, to catch the advancing Soviet forces from the rear. But Hausser was not able to follow the order because units of *Das Reich* and *Leibstandarte* were at that moment entrenched in defensive positions to the east and northeast of Kharkov; in particular, the *Leibstandarte SS 'Adolf Hitler'* was facing practically on its own attacks by the Soviet 3rd Tank Army on both sides of Tschugujew and the *Das Reich* was fighting in the Woltschansk sector against the bulk of the Soviet 69th Army. On February 5, the 1st Soviet Guards Army captured Izyum, just to the rear of *Heeresgruppe*

Don, threatening to cut the German supply lines. The next day, in an emergency meeting at Rastenburg, Hitler, though reluctant, ordered von Manstein to withdraw Hoth's *4.Panzer-Armee* and *Armee-Abteilung Hollidt* across the Mius. To the north of Kharkov, Bjelogorod fell into Soviet hands. *Armee-Abteilung Lanz* was ordered to form an assault group in the area southeast of Kharkov to prevent a new Soviet breakthrough towards Nowomoskowsk. That group was to be formed with *Totenkopf* units and was to reach the Poltava sector. At the same time, the *SS-Pz.Korps* had been given the order to hold a front a hundred kilometers long, facing three Soviet armies, and was to mount an attack to the south towards Losowaja. To carry out that mission, Hausser's corps also needed *Totenkopf* troops, and at any rate at least ten days were needed until its hundred and twenty railway convoys could reach their destination. At that moment, the only unit available was the *SS-Kradschützen-Regiment Thule*, which after having assembled at Poltava, was forthwith attached to the *SS-Pz.Korps*. On February 10, despite Soviet attacks along the entire front, the overall situation did not appear catastrophic for the Germans; in fact, *1.Pz.Armee* still held Slawjansk and *Armee-Abt. Hollidt* had been able to withdraw behind the Mius. Also, the Soviets

SS-Ogruf. Paul Hausser.

Waffen-SS half-tracks moving across the steppe, 1943.

were convinced that the Germans were on the verge of preparing a general retreat behind the Dnieper; according to General Vatutin, the nine German divisions that had just been transferred to the Ukrainian front were there only to cover the withdrawal. This mistaken assessment of the situation of the situation in the field led the Soviets directly into a trap that General von Manstein would soon set for them.

A *PzKpfw IV Ausf. G* followed by a *PzKpfw III Ausf. J* having just arrived in Poltava, with their muzzles still shrouded (NARA).

A *Marder III*, **February 1943.**

The arrival of the Totenkopf units

On February 12, the leading elements of *SS-Pz.Rgt.3* reached Poltava: strangely, despite the seriousness of the situation and the shortage of armored units in the front line, the tanks of *I./SS-Pz.Rgt.3* lay idle for more than a week at the railway station. The German headquarters likely wanted to wait for all of the units of the division to assemble before committing them to the battle. On the morning of the same day, the *I./Thule* began its march to Krasnograd. Meanwhile, other units of the division reached Poltava. In the evening, *III./SS-Pz.Gren.Rgt.1 'T'* reached Kiev. During the night between February 12-13, the last convoys of *I./SS-*

Pz.Rgt.3 reached Poltava; the unit began its march in the early morning hours. More than seventy tanks disappeared in a snowstorm after having crossed the Worskla River. The *II./Thule* reached Krasnograd that day, quickly establishing positions along the defensive line on the outskirts of the city. At that time, all of the recon patrols had returned without having encountered any enemy units; throughout the sector, the roads were completely empty. Information provided by several local peasants revealed that the Soviet soldiers had ordered the evacuation of most of the villages throughout the region and had used the civilian population to ensure their supply of fuel, forcing the locals to work for them.

SS-Hstuf. Meierdress's PzKpfw III 'I01' at Tschugujew.

General Hubert Lanz.

In the Kharkov sector meanwhile, the situation continued to become ever more critical for the *SS-Pz.Korps* which was being attacked by three full Soviet armies. Encirclement of the city was now imminent. *SS-Ogruf.* Paul Hausser then gave the order to prepare to blow the bridges and to mine the roads in anticipation of the evacuation of Kharkov. General Lanz, in accordance with Hitler's directives, halted all of these preparations and instead organized the defense of the city. It was in this context that the *Totenkopf* was ordered to send all of its available forces to Walki. The *Totenkopf* then assigned *SS-Stubaf.* Schulze the command of a *Kampfgruppe* consisting of the following elements:

-*Stab and Stabs-Kp. II./SS-Pz.Gren.Rgt.1 "T"*
- *4. and 5.Kp/SS-Pz.Gren.Rgt.1 "T"*

- 14.(Fla)Kp./SS-Pz.Gren.Rgt.1 "T"
- I./SS-Art.Rgt.3 "T"
- SS-StuG-Abt.3 "T" (minus one battery)

The *Kampfgruppe* began its march towards Walki on the evening of February 14. That same day, *Armee-Abteilung Lanz* was subordinated to *Heeresgruppe Don*, which was subsequently renamed *Heeresgruppe Sud*. The German command had to deal with a sudden thaw, which transformed the entire Ukrainian front into an immense bog. Because of the mud, *IV./SS-Art.Rgt.3 'T'* took four days to cover the three hundred kilometers that separated Kiev from Poltava. The march of other German units also met with strong delays because of the wretched state of the ground and all of that seriously compromised the preparations for the future counteroffensive.

Also on February 14, General Lanz discussed the Führer's orders and the general situation with *SS-Ogruf.* Hausser.

A *Totenkopf* grenadier, February 1943.

It now seemed impossible to plug the gap to the west of Kharkov and the Soviet 6th Army was on the verge of cutting the Krasnograd-Kharkov railway line, which was an indispensable artery for the survival of the *Armee-Abteilung*. Faced with this alarming situation, von Manstein orderd the *Totenkopf* to regroup at Walki from where it could either wipe out the Soviet troops west of Kharkov or attack to the south to block the enemy advance towards Krasnograd.

Totenkopf **armored troops, overtaking a column of infantry, February 1943.**

The *SS-Panzer-Korps* was ordered not to send its messages directly to the *SS-FHA* without first going through normal army channels, officially so as to not create confusion.

The evacuation of Kharkov

Despite the gravity of the situation, Hitler repeated his order to hold Kharkov at all costs. With the 3rd Tank Army of Lieutenant General Rybalko which was advancing from Osnovo, the Germans had only a narrow corridor barely ten kilometers wide through which they could withdraw. Inside Kharkov were troops of the *Grossdeutschland* who were defending the western edge of the city, those of *Das Reich* who defended the northern suburbs, those of the *Leibstandarte* that defended the eastern suburbs and the 320.Inf.Div. defending the southeastern sector. To the northwest, contact with *Korps Raus* had been lost; *Armee-Abteilung Lanz* had in the meantime already issued orders to destroy the supply depots and military installations. *SS-Ogruf.* Paul Hausser then requested General Lanz to authorize the evacuation of Kharkov by 16:30, otherwise he would give the order himself. The

Waffen-SS **troops abandoning Kharkov, February 1943.**

commander of the *SS-Pz.Korps* also reported that there were early signs of revolt in the city and that Ukrainian civilians had begun to fire upon German soldiers. Lanz confirmed

Hitler's order, that was, to hold Kharkov to the last man. Nevertheless, Paul Hauuser stuck to his decision and informed *Armee-Abteilung Lanz* and *Korps Raus* of his intention to abandon Kharkov during the night between February 14-15 and to have the *SS-Pz.Korps* withdraw to the other side of the Udy River, in total contradiction to the orders of his *Führer*. General Lanz, aware of going against Hitler's directive but convinced of the correctness of Paul Hausser's decision, delayed transmitting it to his superiors.

An *SdKfz.251 Ausf C* of the *4./SS-Pz.Gr.Rgt.1* as part of *SS-Kampfgruppe Schulze* on the march, still lacking its winter livery. (NA)

A column of *Marders* of *SS-Pz.Jg.Abt. 'T'* moving to the front.

He knew, in fact, that once operations for the evacuation of Kharkov had been put in motion, it would not be possible to stop them. The *Totenkopf* had to send another *Kampgruppe* to Walki, which was formed on February 15 at Krasnograd, using the *II./SS-Krad.Rgt. Thule*, a battery from *SS-Art.Rgt.3 'T'*, a battery from *SS-StuG-Abt.3 'T'*, an anti-tank platoon and a motorcycle platoon. In the Krasnograd sector, *I./Thule* established contact with the *Das Reich* motorcycle battalion at Meleschkowka, setting up the basis for von Manstein's counteroffensive. Meanwhile, fighting had begun in the streets of Kharkov. The lone corridor to the southwest still remained as an escape route, which in the meantime had shrunk to a width of only two kilometers.

A *Pak 38* on the outskirts of Kharkov. (*Preussischer Kultur Besitz*)

German motorized troops with a sidecar and a *Kettenkrad*.

The pressure exerted by the Soviets was very strong. The *Das Reich* troops had aleady begun to withdraw from the northern suburbs. Intense fighting flared up in the eastern part of the city between Soviet troops and the SS grenadiers. From his command post, *SS-Gruf.* Hausser was undecided; he had no desire at all to sacrifice his men uselessly. At 13:00 on February 15, 1943, aware that the *Totenkopf* troops would not make it in time to lend their support, Hausser gave the order to evacuate the city. This act of insubordination caused great amazement in German military circles because it came from a high-ranking *Waffen SS* commander. The *Führer* was, however, not upset by Hausser's behavior, probably because he considered the advantages stemming from the new situation: the entire SS corps had been preserved and was ready to attack with the support of the *Grossdeutschland* and the *320.Infanterie-Division*. In addition, the Soviets continued to believe that the real German intention was to withdraw across the Dnieper; to that end, the Stavka ordered the 6th Army and the *'Popov'* armored group to make a rapid push to the Dnieper, without worrying about covering their flanks.

Totenkopf half-tracks and assault guns on the Ukrainian steppe. (NA)

Soviet infantry rushing to attack in the streets of Kharkov.

Preparations for the counteroffensive

During the day of February 15, *SS-Kampfgruppe Schulze* arrived in the Kowjagi-Wyssokopolje-Kolomak area, while II./*Thule* reached Walki shortly after noon. The situation continued to be difficult for *Heeresgruppe Süd* because to the west of Kharkov the Soviets had decided to launch their 40th Army towards Achtyrka. This advance constituted a threat, but at the same time the German command breathed a sigh of relief because the Soviets did not head south against the sector where the units of the *SS-Pz.Korps* were assembling for the counteroffensive. Von Manstein took advantage of Hitler's visit to his headquarters at Zaporozhe on February 17, 1943 to convince him not to think of recapturing Kharkov right away, but to first eliminate the threat that faced them on the Dnieper. Von Manstein wanted to first block the enemy advance and then to attack the flanks of the Soviet armies, between Kharkov and Slawjansk.

A *T-34* with Soviet infantry aboard in the Kharkov.

Paul Hausser on board a tank.

General Erich von Manstein.

Once that victory had been achieved, his armored divisions would then be able to quickly surround Kharkov with a vast encircling maneuver from the north. The spearhead of this new counteroffensive was to be the *SS-Pz.Korps*. That same day, *SS-Ogruf.* Paul Hausser issued an order of the day to thank his men for the efforts they had made:

"...*From January 30, the armored Corps, in changing conditions of attack and defense, has stopped the assault of three Soviet armies and inflicted many casualties upon them. An entire cavalry corps was destroyed almost to the last man...For the first time, the* Leibstandarte *and* Das Reich *armored grenadier divisions, along with the* Totenkopf, *were able to fight shoulder to shoulder. Each specialty gave the best of itself during these weeks and despite the confusion caused by grouping these units together, a confusion which complicated the tasks of the commanders, a decisive defensive victory was achieved*".

In the meantime, at Walki, *SS-Kampfgruppe Schulze* and the *II./Thule* were placed under the command of *SS-Ostubaf.* Lammerding, thus forming *SS-Kampfgruppe Lammerding*. That group had been given the order to secure the northern flank of the coming counteroffensive and to oppose the advance of the Soviet 3rd Tank Army.

Totenkopf half-tracks and assault guns on the move. (NARA)

A *Marder* and other vehicles in a Ukrainian village, 1943.

The *Thule* regiment was temporarily detache from the division. Its mobility and its firepower constituted a significant reinforcement for *Korps Raus*. Towards evening, *SS-Kampfgruppe Schulze* was able to establish contact with the *Grossdeutschland* in the area to the east of Udamyj. Meanwhile, *II./Thule* reached the line Nowyj Mertschik-Swch.Kirassirkij. As of February 17, most of the *Totenkopf* convoys were still stalled between Kiev and Poltava. With Kharkov recaptured, the Soviets continued their attacks: in the breach that had been opened between the *1.Panzerarmee* and the southern wing of *Armee-Abteilung Lanz*, defended by the *Leibstandarte*, they threw their 6th Army towards the Dnieper, seizing Pavlograd and threatening the section of the railway line that led to Dniepropetrovsk. To rapidly eliminate that threat, von Manstein decided to throw the *SS-Pz.Korps* into a counterattack from the area of Krasnograd towards Pavlograd; the SS corps was then supposed, in cooperation with the *4.Panzerarmee* (*XLVIII.Pz.Korps* and *LVII.Pz.Korps*) to destroy the enemy forces that had broken into the gap. Conduct of the operations on the left flank was logically assigned to *4.Panzerarmee* under *Generaloberst* Hoth, because *Armee-Abteilung Lanz* was not able to contemporaneously assume the management of the counterattack as well as defense of the sectors located to the west and southwest of Kharkov.

Elements of *Kampfgruppe Schulze* moving across the Ukrainian steppe. (NARA)

General Erhard Raus. (BDC)

On February 18, the vanguard of the Soviet 6th Army got to within one hundred kilometers of Zaporozhe, threatening the entire German defensive front in that region. It thus became necessary for the Totenkopf to speed up the regrouping of its units in the Poltava area in order to be able to be quickly committed to the imminent counteroffensive.

Counterattack by the SS-Pz.Korps

On February 19, *Heeresgruppe Süd* ordered the *4.Panzerarmee* to go on the counterattack towards Pereschtschepino, Pavlograd and Grischino in order to wipe out Soviet forces that were nearing the Dnieper. The *Das Reich* was to hit the flank of the Soviet troops who were advancing to the west and the *Totenkopf* was to be employed behind it. That same day fresh units continued to arrive in the Poltava sector. Around 4:00, to the north of Ljubotin and at Olschany, the Soviets attacked the positions of *SS-Kampfgruppe Lammerding*. On its right flank, *SS-Kampfgruppe Schulze* was pushed back to the line Ivanschtschenkov-Staryj Mertschik. At 8:30 a Soviet infantry regiment attacked Nowyj Mertschik, which was defended only by the *7.Kp./Thule*; in the fighting that followed, the SS troops suffered heavy losses. In the afternoon, elements of *Grossdeutschland* and of the *Thule* regiment counterattacked, forcing the Soviets to abandon part of Nowyj Mertschik.

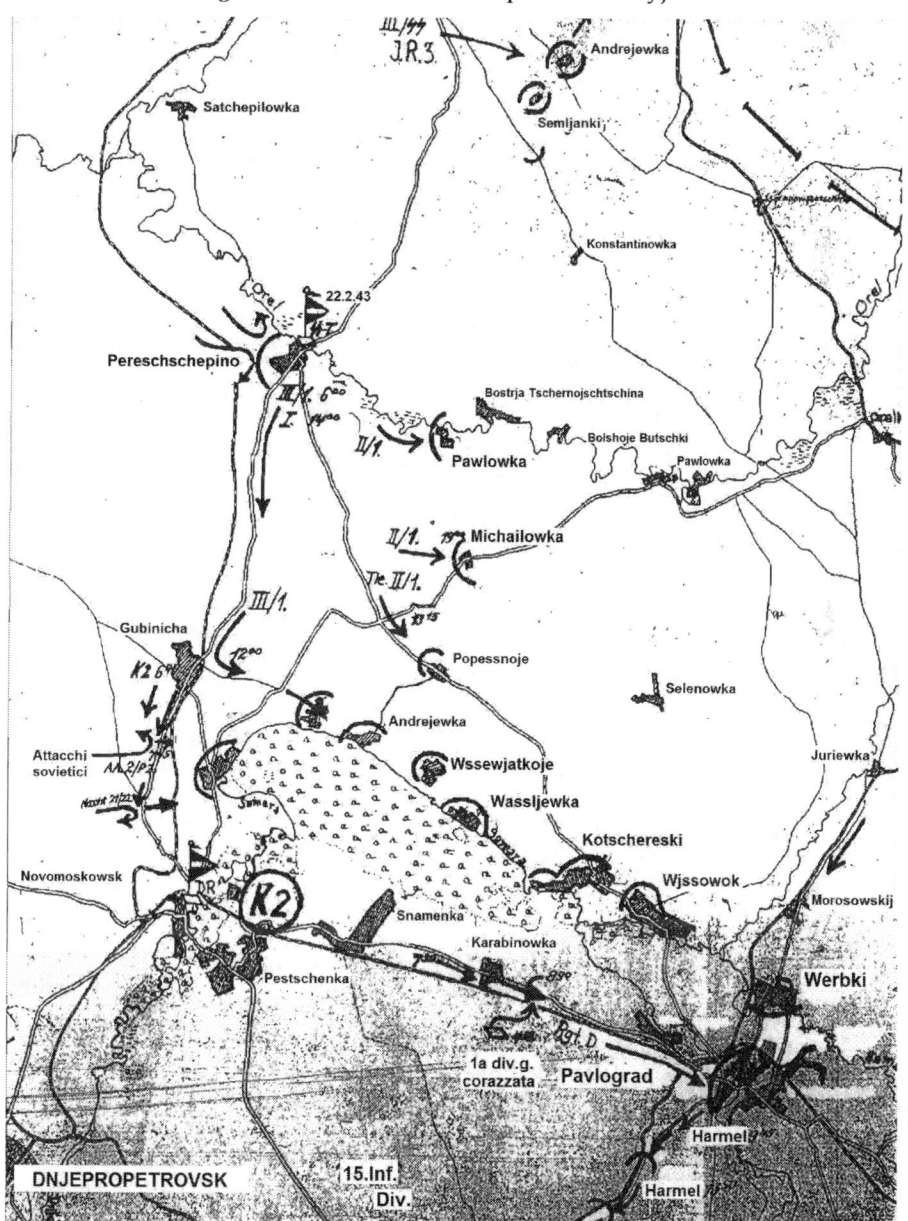

The area involved in the fighting between 19 and 22 February.

At the same time, *SS-Kampfgruppe Schulze* was able to force the Soviets to abandon part of Stary Mertschik. At Bairak, the situation still remained tenuous for the *II./Thule* and losses of SS troops were very high; *SS-Stubaf.* Georg Bochmann, the battalion commander, was seriously wounded in the fighting. Also on February 19, General Lanz was replaced at the head of his *Armee-Abteilung* by General Werner Kempf, officially effective as of February 21. On February 20, the *II./Thule*, along with the *Aufkl.-Abt. 'GD'*, attacked and routed the Soviet troops that were between Dobropolje and Nowyj Mertschik.

Half-tracks of *SS-Art.Rgt. Totenkopf* with guns in tow.

In the *SS-Pz.Korps* offensive sector, after having captured Pereschtschepino, troops of *Das Reich* crossed the Orel River and continued their attack to the south, breaking into the right flank of the Soviet 6th Army. At 10:40 the *Totenkopf* was subordinated to the *SS-Pz.Korps* and was ordered to reach the Krasnograd - Karlowka sector. The *I./SS-Pz.Rgt.3* then began its march to move to Poltava, reaching Karlovka on the morning of 21 February. During the night between February 20-21, precisely at 3:00, *Das Reich* crossed the Samara River and began to attack Pavlograd, beginning at 13:30. Its attack shattered the spearhead of the Soviet offensive towards the Dnieper, thus cutting off the forward elements of the Soviet 6th Army from their rear area. Around

A Totenkopf PzKpfw III. (BA)

noontime, the *SS-Pz.Korps* and the *Totenkopf* were attached to *4.Panzerarmee* while the *Leibstandarte* was subordinated to *Armee-Abteilung Kempf*. To eliminate the strong concentrations of enemy troops that were east of the line Krasnograd-Nowomoskowsk, the intervention of fresh units was needed. At 10:30 the *Totenkopf* was ordered to clear the road that ran from Krasnograd as far as the area west of Pereschtschepino.

A *PzKpfw III* of the *Totenkopf* on the move, February 1943.

Tiger "401" in the Pereschtschepno area. (*Bundesarchiv*)

Once that location had been reached, *SS-Pz.Rgt.3* and *SS-Pz.Gren.Rgt.1 'T'* were to attack Pavlograd from the north, supporting the *Das Reich* troops who were to move from the west. *SS-Pz.Gren.Rgt.3 'T'* was to advance towards the area to the east of Pereschtschepino and seize the stretch of railway line situated to the north of Pavlograd to prevent the Soviets from getting any reinforcements through. Some *Totenkopf* elements thus reached the area to relieve the bulk of the *Das Reich* southeast of Krasnograd and at Otradowka. At the same time, the divison's reconnaissance group, attacking southwards from the area of Jeremejewska, wiped out an entire Soviet infantry battalion. *SS-Pz.Rgt.3* had a rough time reaching its assigned sector because of the frozen roads and the inexperience of the tank crews. On February 22, while the *Totenkopf* attack groups were assembling at Pereschtschepino with the temperature at minus twenty degrees, the 106th Rifle Brigade attacked the village, taking advantage of the thick mist that enveloped the plain. Defending the positions were the grenadiers of *III./SS.Pz.Gren.Rgt.1 'T'*, who were able to drive off the enemy riflemen, thanks to effective support by a number of *Flakvierling*: the Soviets left at least 150 dead on the ground and about sixty prisoners fell into German hands. At 11:30, *SS-Pz.Gren.Rgt.1 'T'* under *SS-Stubaf*. Otto Baum arrived to reinforce Pereschtschepino, followed shortly by tanks of *SS-Pz.Rgt.3* coming from Poltava.

Totenkopf **grenadiers and** *PzKpfw III* **tanks during a transfer march.**

An *MG-42* **mounted on a German** *Waffen SS* **half-track. (NA)**

As soon as they arrived, the SS troops were subjected to a new attack by an entire Soviet infantry battalion. Once again, German firepower inflicted heavy losses on the Soviets. The *MG-42* machine guns, with their formidable rate of fire of 1,500 rounds per minute, cut down the attackers by the score. The Soviet soldiers who had escaped death withdrew. But their Calvary was not yet over: *SS-Stubaf*. Baum decided to pursue them. The SS soldiers climbed aboard their half-tracks and drove across the steppe. As soon as they spotted any fleeing Soviet soldiers, they slaughtered them in a matter of minutes with fire from their machine guns. At 13:15, *II./SS-Pz.Gren.Rgt.1 'T'* coming from Mertschik went on the attack, with the objective of taking Pavlograd from the northwest. The Soviet defensive positions were overrun. However, a cavalry unit arrived and threatened the right flank of the SS troops to the west of Popasnoje. During the course of the day, contact was made with a patrol from the *Leibstandarte* at Alexandrowka, southeast of Krasnograd. The *III./SS-Pz.Gren.Rgt.2 LSSAH* had been ordered to establish contact with the *Totenkopf* at Otrada. To the south, *Das Reich* was able to make contact with *XLVIII.Pz.Korps* east of Pavlograd.

Two *StuG III* of the *Totenkopf* during a halt in the Pavlograd area. (NA)

Around 14:00 on February 22, several tanks from *Totenkopf* repulsed an enemy attack against Pereschtschepino supported by tanks. At the cost of heavy losses, the enemy was driven back and thrown across the other side of the railway line to the west. The villages in the valley northwest of Pereschtschepino, however, remained in Soviet hands. During the night between February 22-23, around 1:00, the *Totenkopf* went on the attack, moving southeasterly from the line Andrejewka, Popasnoje, Michailowka and Pavlovka. On the right flank, *SS-Pz.Gren.1 'T'* encountered tough going in the Andrejeka sector: only its Third Battalion managed to advance along the course of the Samara River. The march of the SS troops was slowed mainly by the condition of the terrain, which had been transformed into a bog because of the sudden thaw. Around 5:00, the Soviet troops that were entrenched in the area around Andrejewka were wiped out and the SS troops attacked and seized Wassiljewka. The *15.(Kradsch.)Kp./SS-Pz.Gren.Rgt.1 'T'*, led by *SS-Hstuf.* Emil Stürzbecher, was then able to penetrate the Soviet lines at Popasnoje and continued on towards Kotschereschki, where several Soviet motorcycle units were cut to pieces.

Grenadiers and a *StuG III*. (NA)

Elements of *2.(gep.)/SS-Pz.Gr.Rgt.1* in the Pereschtschepino area, February 1943. (NARA)

A *Waffen-SS* artillery piece opens fire against the enemy.

Soviet Guards cavalry troops at the gallop across the steppe.

An enemy infantry battalion was destroyed in the fighting inside the village of Kotschereschki by *III./SS-Pz.Gren.Rgt.1 'T'*. The advance of the SS troops stalled in front of Wjasowok, where elements of the 267th Rifle Division and of the 19th Tank Brigade had dug in well, geeting the attackers with a horrific wall of fire. One hill, situated north of the village, had been fortified and constituted an excellent observation point for their artillery. Progress was also made difficult by fire from Soviet artillery coming from the southern bank of the Samara. *II./SS-Pz.Gren.Rgt.1 'T'* then attempted to dislodge the Soviets; fighting went on until late at night without any results. This lack of success prevented the *Totenkopf* division from achieving its objectives, in particular, that of making contact with troops of the *Das Reich* division in the area of Pavlograd. On the left flank, *I./SS-Pz.Gren.Rgt.3 'T'* left Krasnograd at 6:00, moving to the south. Around 14:00, patrols reported that villages in the Orel Valley, as far as Tschernoglasowka, had been abandoned by the enemy. At the end of the day, the division reported the number of tanks it had available to the *SS-Pz.Korps*: 62 *PzKpfw III*, 18 *PzKpfw IV*, 9 *PzKpfw VI Tiger*. Not a single tank had been lost in combat, but breakdowns and accidents had significantly reduced the number of operational vehicles. In the *Korps z.b.V. Raus* sector, the *II./Thule* was engaged in defending the line Perebudowa-Krasnoje Snamia. At 8:40,

Grossdeutschland reported to the Corps: "...*Situation uncertain within the SS troops who have no contact on their right flank*". In fact, less than an hour later the Soviets, who were increasingly capable of determining the weak points in the German defenses, broke into the Grossdeutschland positions at Pschtschenkowa, thereby threatening the rear area of I./*Thule*. The SS battalion then was ordered by the *Korps z.b.V.* to withdraw to Alexejewa in order to form a blocking line between Panassowka and Trudoljubowka. Further south, the *XL.Pz.Korps* had broken the resistance of the *'Popov'* armored group and advanced over a wide front to the northeast, on both sides of the Barwenkowa.

German grenadiers moving into a village after having destroyed several tanks.

An armored car commander.

On February 24, the *Totenkopf* resumed its attack to seize the crossing points over the Samara at Werbki. The division was also tasked with taking Orelka so that it could later continue on to Losowaja. The *Totenkopf* gathered its forces in preparation for the attack: the *I.(gep.)/SS-Pz.Rgt.1 'T'* was recalled from Perschtschepino along with *SS-Pz.Rgt.3*. The *Totenkopf* tanks experienced difficulty in reaching their departure points. The bulk of the division ended up attacking around 9:30. *II./SS-Pz.Rgt.1 'T'*, supported by several tanks, attacked Wjassowok and systematically cleared out Soviet strongpoints, one after another. The city was completely seized at 13:45. The division's armored group, preceded by a formidable artillery barrage, attacked in two successive waves and cleaned out the heights to the north and northwest of the city, inflicting heavy losses on the Soviet infantry which had made the mistake of fleeing over open ground after having held out doggedly against the SS grenadiers. The *II./SS-Pz.Gren.Rgt.1 'T'* exploited this success and continued on towards Werbki, along the railway line, in order to strike from behind the Soviet units that were facing *Das Reich*.

Tanks and half-tracks halted while waiting for orders to attack. (NARA)

Totenkopf **Panzers attacking a village. (NARA)**

Meanwhile, the *Totenkopf Panzergruppe* had been able to establish a bridgehead on the Ternowka River at 14:00. *SS-Ostubaf.* Baum proceeded towards Morosowsky and Werbki, making contact with elements of the *Das Reich* division. The meeting between forward elements of *Das Reich* and of *Totenkopf* was characterized by several incidents involving *"identification"* caused by the presence of many enemy formations on the battlefield. One of these incidents occurred when *Totenkopf* troops opened fire on several *Das Reich* vehicles. Via radio, those vehicles quickly warned their comrades: *"Do not fire. We are the leading element of the Das Reich!"*. The *Totenkopf* soldiers replied sarcastically: *"Don't worry. We only shoot at important targets"*. After having captured the crossings over the Samara, the Das Reich was able to continue its attack northward towards Losowaja. At Werbki, the *Totenkopf* had destroyed about a dozen enemy tanks, but its own losses

The Axis Forces

were also notable, especially with regard to the tanks. Many of the tank crews were missing, but were found a few days later by personnel of the repair company. After having covered the division's northern flank, *SS-Pz.Gren.Rgt.3 'T'* was heavily engaged between Seleny-Rai and Magdenkowa, where it wiped out several Soviet units. Shortly after, it regrouped in the Orelka sector. In late afternoon of the same day, *SS-Aufkl.-Abt.3 'T'* reported the capture of Orelka. By these actions the *Totenkopf* consolidated the northern flank of the *SS-Pz.Korps* and the situation turned particularly favorable for the continuation of the offensive to the northeast. Around evening, the *SS-Pz.Korps* was able to report that enemy forces to the north and south of the Samara had been wiped out.

A *PzKpfw III* with grenadiers aboard. (NARA)

New Soviet attacks

In the *Korps z.b.V. Raus* sector, *SS-Rgt. Thule* was heavily committed: the *I./Thule* had to deal with attacks by two Soviet infantry regiments. After having taken Shelestowo, *I./Thule* continued on as far as Iskrowka, which the *Grossdeutschland* reconnaissance group also reached. The capture of those two places completely stalled the Soviet offensive. The crisis situation to the west of Kharkov seemed to have passed. During the last few days, the attacks by the *SS-Pz.Korps* had enabled the gap that separated it from *Heeresgruppe Süd* to be shut.

Waffen-SS **grenadiers and Panzers during an attack.**

But the Soviets did not stay still: on February 25, the 25th Guards Army and the 6th Army advanced to the southwest between Kharkov and Slavjansk; *4.Panzerarmee* was called upon to face off against five full armored corps. To prevent the Soviets from bringing in fresh forces from the east and northeast, the *XLVIII.Pz.Korps* had to attack to the north, while the *SS-Pz.Korps* had to push to the northeast towards the Donetz. On the corps' right flank, the *Das Reich* was to attack towards Losowaja. On the right flank, the *Totenkopf* was ordered to attack towards Panjutina. The rear areas of the two SS divisions were to be covered by the *15.Infanterie-Division*. Nevertheless, Soviet units that had been cut off by the attack of the two SS divisions caused significant problems along the road along which supplies for the *SS-Pz.Korps* passed: on the morning of February 25, Soviet elements cut the *Totenkopf* supply line at Nageshdowka and attacked the *SS-Pz.Rgt.3* logistics train. All available units in the Kotschereschki area were thrown into a counterattack and what was left of the Soviet troops fled to the northeast. In the meantime, the bulk of the *Totenkopf* had gone on the attack. At 10:00, the division's armored group, consisting of *I.(gep.)SS-Pz.Gren.Rgt.1 'T'* and *SS-Pz.Rgt.3* moved towards Panjutina from the western bank of the Ternowka River.

Grenadiers on the attack. (NARA)

Troops of Baum's *I.(gep.)/SS-Pz.Gren.Rgt.1 'T'* attacking against Wjassowok.

SS-Pz.Gren.Rgt.1 'T' moved nothwards from Orelka, facing numerous enemy formations supported by *T-34* tanks. Spurred on by their political commissars, the Soviet soldiers fought spiritedly, slowing the advance of the SS grenadiers and then withdrawing to the north after having inflicted heavy losses on the SS troops. Worried about the number of losses, *SS-Staf.* Becker set his troops in pursuit of the enemy, ordering the utmost caution.

Tiger '423' of *4.(schw.)/SS-Pz.Rgt.3*.

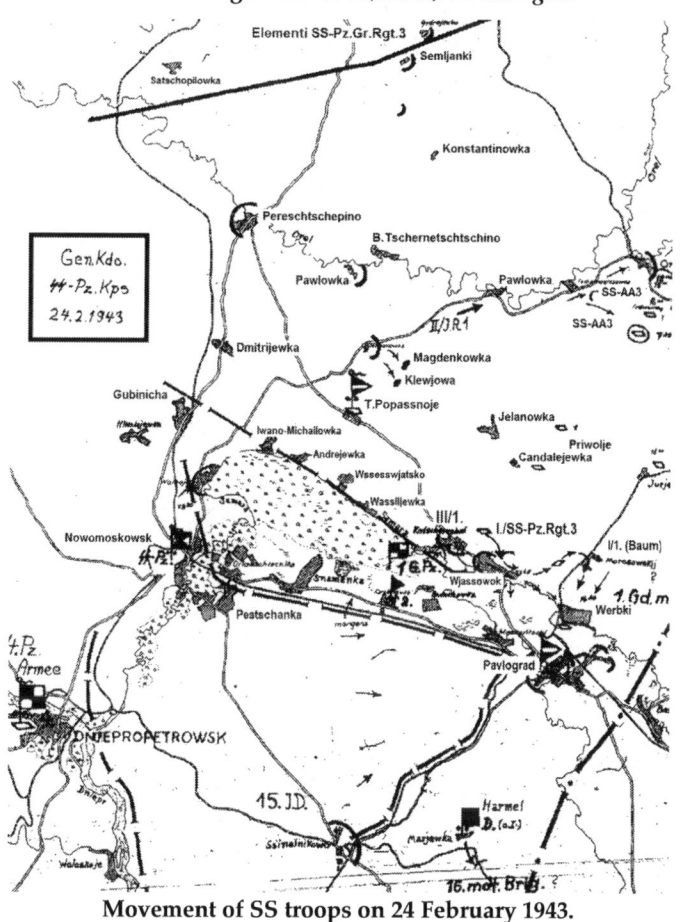

SS-Ostubaf. Baum.

Movement of SS troops on 24 February 1943.

It was then that Theodor Eicke arrived on the scene in his *Fieseler Storch*. His presence buoyed the morale of the troops, who resumed the attack with great enthusiasm. Preceded by Walter Bestmann's scouts, the SS troops quickly seized Pokrowskoje and Fedorowka. *Angriffgruppe Leiner* of *SS-Pz.Gren.Rgt.3 'T'* was, however, stalled in the area west of Kondratjewka, not being able to eliminate the enemy defenses until around 12:30 and then continuing its march towards Panjutina. The *Totenkopf* engineer battalion was engaged in heavy fighting with the enemy in the area to the southwest of Nageschdowka. In the early afternoon, the vanguard of *SS-Pz.Rgt.3* reached the outskirts of Alexejewa: the *Totenkopf* tanks were blocked by violent fire unleashed by Soviet anti-tank guns that were well dug in behind a ditch south of the village. When some *T-34* tanks suddenly appeared, a furious battle flared up. This time, the SS armored units got the worst of it and *SS-Stubaf.* Leiner was forced to order a withdrawal as he was short of fuel and ammunition. Around 16:00, *III./SS-Pz.Gren.Rgt.1 'T'* clashed with another Soviet formation of about a thousand men in the Jelenowka-Sergejewka sector.

A *StuG III* and other vehicles crossing through a Ukrainian village, February 1943.

Grossdeutschland **grenadiers.**

Soon after, the *SS-Pz.Korps* chief of staff, *Oberstleutnant* i.G. Müller, issued the following order: *"Priority mission: wipe out enemy forces south of Orelka, also attacking by night"*. The *Totenkopf* was to prevent any Soviet penetrations to the northeast. During the previous day, the division had destroyed twenty-two tanks and two armored cars. During the night between the 25th and 26th, the Soviets attempted to withdraw from the sector that was to the south or Orelka, taking advantage of darkness. The *6.Kp./SS-Pz.Rgt.3* was sent towards Losowaja with its fifteen *PzKpfw III* tanks, with orders to capture the road situated to the west of the city. There was no initial reconnaissance and Biermeier had to attack without infantry or artillery support. His company suffered heavy losses because of the incoherent orders issued by *SS-Stubaf.* Leiner. Lost in the dark, he clashed with several *T-34* tanks accompanied by cavalry troopers north of Strastnoj. During the fierce battle that ensued, three enemy tanks were knocked out and the Soviets lost at least a hundred men. The SS troops also took casualties: within the Third Platoon alone there were twenty dead, while the crew of tank "634" was missing. When the soldiers of the company went to look after the immobilized tanks and their crews, they found that all of their comrades had been massacred by Soviet soldiers and that several corpses had also been horribly mutilated.

February 24: *Totenkopf SdKfz.251* **half-tracks, loaded with grenadiers, moving to the northeast, passing through Marinskoje and Nikolajewka.**

SS grenadiers and tanks.

On February 26, the *SS-Pz.Korps* was ordered to capture Losowaja, a key position in the Soviet defenses of that sector of the front. The *Totenkopf* was to eliminate the danger that weighed over its rear area, continuing its attacks to the north, towards Panjutina. After having left Wassiljewka during the morning, the *15.(Kradsch.)Kp./SS-Pz.Gren.1 'T'* soon had an encounter with a Soviet logistic support battalion which was absolutely in no shape to face a fight. The SS motorcyclists took ninety-two prisoners and captured a large quantity of equipment. The *II./SS-Pz.Gren.Rgt.1 'T'* was instead engaged against a strong enemy force at Sergejewka, putting it to flight. Continuing its advance, the SS unit destroyed another two Soviet battalions in the area between Jelenowka and Priwolje. The Soviet troops who had pulled back to the Tschernoglasowka sector were eliminated in close-quarter fighting. To the south of Orelka the fighting lasted deep into the night. This situation had repercussions on the offensive by the *Totenkopf*, which had to commit two of its battalions to eliminate the Soviet units that were seeking to cross the Orel.

The death of Theodor Eicke

For its part, *SS-Pz.Rgt.3* attempted to force a crossing over the Orel River north of Strasnoj. At around ten in the morning, the SS panzers ran up against a solid wall of anti-tank guns and *T-34* tanks at Zaredarowka, situated northwest of Losowaja. Many tanks hit by enemy fire and were abandoned along the railway embankment. Facing them were the tanks of the 1st Guards Tank Army, which had been sorely tested during the preceding weeks and which had only about fifty tanks still running! The tank battle raged on, but the division headquarters was unaware of the exact location of the clashes. Worried about the fate of his son-in-law, *SS-Stubaf.* Leiner, Eicke decided to carry out an aereial reconnaissance in order to take stock of the situation himself. He climbed aboard his *Fieseler Storch*, accompanied by his aide, *SS-Hstuf.* Otto Friedrich. The pilot of the plane was *Oberfeldwebel* Michael Werner. Around 13:00, Eicke stopped off at the forward command post of a recon group, where he was received by *SS-Ustuf.* Kohlig who informed him that Zaderowka was still in Soviet hands. The Soviets had established roadblocks along the road and had *T-34* tanks. Eicke ignored the report and took off shortly afterwards. He then reached troops of the reconnaissance group that were in an even more forward position to the northeast of Orelka. His *Fieseler Storch* used a small field to land in: the scouts had no information of the whereabouts of the armored regiment because radio contact had not yet been re-established. The plane took off yet again to search for the panzers. It was seen around

Himmler, Heinz Lammerding and Theodor Eicke.

***Waffen-SS* recon troops entering a village.**

Two *StuG III* attacking in a snowstorm. (NARA)

16:00 by soldiers from the division to the south of Artelnoje: *"We saw several anti-aircraft rounds explode near the aircraft. The Fieseler Storch caught fire and began to fall to the ground in front of the enemy positions between Artelnoje and Michailowka"*. And thus died tragically the commander of the *Totenkopf*, Theodor Eicke. News of his death spread quickly.

Theodor Eicke inspecting the front lines with *SS-Hstuf*. Friedrich.

A *PzKpfw III* providing security for a supply column.

SS-Ogruf. Paul Hausser immediately advised Himmler by telegram. Himmler in turn informed Hitler. The official announcement of his death was delayed until 1 March, because the *Reichsführer-SS* wanted all the details of the incident before informing the press. His death was acted out like a drama within the *Totenkopf*. Despite his harsh methods, he was much beloved by his soldiers, who called him *"papa Eicke"*, with whom he shared their rations and their sacrifices. Even though not a competent military commander, Eicke made up for his lack of training and tactics by his great deterination. *SS-Obf*. Max Simon took his place as commander of the division; command of his regiment in turn was turned over to Otto Baum. Command of the *I.(gep.)/SS-Pz.Gren.Rgt.1 'T'* was assumed by *SS-Hstuf*. Walter Reder. The bodies of Eicke, Otto Friedrich and the pilot, Werner, were picked up the next day by an assault squad from the *Totenkopf* division.

The fighting resumes

On February 27, attacks resumed along the entire front, but the Soviets continued to defend their positions strenuously, in particular at Losowaja and Panjutina. Headquarters 4.*Panzerarmee* ordered the *Totenkopf* to encircle the Soviet forces, attacking north of Losowaja. The *Das Reich* was ordered to destroy the enemy forces concentrated in the Losowaja-Panjutina sector and to pursue them northwards in order to push them against the *Totenkopf* positions. In the early morning hours, *SS-Kampfgruppe Leiner* was able to seize Zaredarowka, continuing its advance toards Panjutina. At 11:35, Gruppe Baum encircled Panjutina from the north and in the afternoon the city began to be attacked by its grenadiers. Despite tank support, the SS grenadiers did not reach the center of the city until evening and each enemy position had to be eliminated with hand grenades. The Soviet infantrymen gave up the fight and attempted to flee northwards: the 15th Rifle Corps had in fact ordered its two divisions to establish a new defensive line to the northwest of Losowaja in an attempt to block the advance of the *SS-Pz.Korps*. But the SS corps had anticipated that movement and had ordered *SS-Pz.Gren.Rgt.3 'T'* to attack towards Krasnopawlowka. Even there, the Soviets defended their positions stubbornly and it was only towards nightfall that the SS grenadiers managed to push the defenders back into the eastern part of the town. The last nests of resistance were eliminated during the night. It was an important success, but the SS losses were high. Towards evening the *Totenkopf* headquarters reported that it still had 112 operational tanks: 61 *PzKpfw III*, 15 *PzKpfw IV*, 9 *PzKpfw VI* and 18 *StuG III*. For its part, the *Das Reich* had finally captured Losowaja while the Soviets withdrew to the northeast.

An *SdKfz.250* of the *Totenkopf* reconnaissance group.

Movement of SS troops on 26 February 1943.

The next day, February 28, the *Totenkopf* set off in pursuit of the Soviets. However, the division was not able to exploit it success, because it was not able to regroup the tanks of *SS-Pz.Rgt.3* that were scattered around the Panjutina sector in time, which delayed the attack of *SS-Pz.Gren.Rgt.1 'T'* towards Jekaterinowka. *SS-Stubaf.* Otto Baum ended up throwing his regiment into the attack without waiting for the support of the armored troops. After having cleaned out the area, the regiment proceded parallel to the course of the Orel and established a bridgehead at Ligowka. Meanwhile, *SS-Pz.Gren.Rgt.3 'T'* eliminated the remaining pockets of enemy resistance at Krasnopawlowka.

Grenadiers and tanks on the march.

The recapture of Kharkov

At the end of February 1943, while *4.Panzerarmee* was attacking southwards, facing the Soviet forces of the 6th and 1st Guards Armies, *Armee-Abteilung Kempf* had carried out a slow withdrawal, continuing to contain the attacks of the Soviet 3rd Tank Army: between February 27-28, that enemy army had gathered around the positions at Kegitschewka and Jefremowka. General Rybalko had in fact decided to send his tanks to the south, against the *SS-Pz.Korps*, to the east of the positions defended by the *Leibstandarte*.

Waffen-SS **Panzers and grenadiers in a Ukrainian village, February 1943.**

SS grenadiers while attacking a village.

A Soviet defensive position on the Ukrainian front, 1943.

A *Marder III* of the *Totenkopf* on the outskirts of a village.

A shortage of sufficient fuel and ammunition, however, forced him to postpone his attack until 3 March. This delay of two days worked to the advantage of the *SS-Pz.Korps* which itself went on the attack on March 1, this time moving to the northwest. The objective was to seize the heights at Bereka and Jefremowka, to align its front with that of the *Leibstandarte*, which was defending the eastern wing of *Armee-Abreilung Kempf*. At that moment, for the first time the *SS-Pz.Korps* had all of its three divisions available for the offensive against Kharkov. In particular, the *Totenkopf* troops were to break through the lines of the 3rd Tank Army near Kegischewka, then to move east and thus cut the Soviet supply lines. At the same time, the *Leibstandarte* and *Das Reich* troops were to make contact further to the north, in the Starowerowka sector. The objective was to encircle the forces of the Soviet 12th and 15th Tank Corps.

On the morning of March 1, *SS-Pz.Gren.Rgt.3 'T'* attacked along the course of the Orel. On the division's right flank, *III./SS-Pz.Gren.Rgt.1 'T'* took Alexejewa following bitter fighting. At 9:20, *I./SS-Pz.Gren.Rgt.1 'T'* followed suit and grenadiers riding on half-tracks were able to capture Oleiniki. On that same day, *SS-Ogruf.* Theodor Eicke, *SS-Hstuf.* Otto Friedrich and *Oberfeldwebel* Werner were buried with full military honors in the cemetery at Otdoschnina. To mark the occasion, *Reichsführer-SS* Himmler decided to bestow the honorific title of *'Theodor Eicke'* to *SS-Pz.Gren.Rgt.3*.

The Axis Forces

The Totenkopf takes the lead

On March 2, the *Totenkopf* was ordered to take Medwedowka; to that purpose, the *Eicke* Regiment moved from Semenowka, while the *Totenkopf* Regiment was to plug the breach between the *SS-Pz.Korps* and the *Leibstandarte*, proceding towards Jeremejewka. The *I./'T'* under *SS-Hstuf.* Reder attacked during the night and captured the station at Schljachowoje; it was an important capture, because the station was on the Krasnograd-Panjutina line, through which supplies passed for the Soviet units that were deployed in Kegitschewka. The loss of Schljachowoje left the Soviets with only a narrow corridor leading to the north, while Reder's troops had gotten to within a few kilometers of Peiper's assault group of the *Leibstandarte*. The fates of the 12th and 15th Tank Corps were practically sealed. Curiously, General Rybalko sent further reinforcements to Kegitschewka, that is to the south, in anticipation of the offensive planned for March 3. Those forces ended up in a pocket after having crossed paths with the retreating forces of the 6th Army, which were fleeing in the opposite direction.

SS-Oberführer **Max Simon.**

Two *Totenkopf* **assault guns entering a village.**

These movements took place in the early hours of the day, when the ground was still frozen, but when the sun began to come out, the mud took over once again. Vehicles were immobilized and fuel and ammunition supplies ceased to arrive. *SS-Pz.Rgt.3* was without fuel until 14:00. Despite this difficult situation, *SS-Pz.Gren.Rgt.1 'T'* was nevertheless able to make its attack at the scheduled hour, around 8:00. *SS-Pz.Gren Rgt.3 'TE'* moved shortly after. At 14:30, Soviet resistance was particularly fierce, with high losses on both sides. At the same time, *I./SS-Pz.Rgt.3* and elements of *Das Reich* were able to make contact with the *Leibstandarte* near Berestowaja. Towards evening, *SS-Pz.Gren Rgt.3 'TE'* in turn was able to make contact with other *Leibstandarte* troops near Kotljarowka.

A *PzKpfw III* with winter livery, on the Ukrainian front.

SS grenadiers engaged in attacking a village, 1943.

The pocket around the Soviet troops in the Jeremejewka area was thus completely shut: more than 50,000 men of the Soviet 3rd Tank army were trapped within it. In the afternoon, the Soviets attempted to open an escape route by attacking to the southeast, in the Paraskowejeske area. However, the bulk of the forces were repulsed and only some elements were able to cross the Orel River and flee to the east, taking advantage of the fact that the *SS-Pz.Korps* did not have enough forces to completely close off the pocket.

During the night between 2 and 3 March, the weather worsened unexpectedly: an intense cold replaced the thaw and strong snowstorms hindered vehicle movement. Shortly after midnight, *SS-Pz.Gren.Rgt.3 'TE'* was subordinated to *Das Reich*, while the rest of the *Totenkopf* was ordered to wipe out Soviet forces in the Losowaja - Kegischewka sector. Meanwhile, other Soviet units tried desperately to escape from the pocket. They were literally cut to pieces by a company of *I./SS-Pz.Rgt.3* and by the engineers of the *Eicke* Regiment. Between 7:00 and 9:00 on March 3, a second enemy group, which was stronger, clashed with an SS combat group consisting of the headquarters and *II.* and *III./'TE'*. The SS grenadiers drove off the Soviets with a counterattack, but *II./'TE'* found itself surrounded at Kotljarowka, where fierce fighting erupted for control of each isba. Kurt Launer's battalion was rescued in the afternoon, thanks to the intervention of *III.(gep.)/Der Führer*. The Soviets then fled to the south. The *I.(gep.)'T'*, moving from Jeremejewka, cut off their escape route, inflicting heavy losses. General Kopstow, commander of the Soviet 15th Tank Corps, was killed during the fighting. His unit fell apart, abandoning all of its tanks and heavy weapons inside the pocket. Only a few isolated groups of soldiers managed to escape. In the meantime, the battle for Jeremejewka continued. The *Totenkopf* Regiment attacked the city from the west: it was necessary to fight from house to house. A Soviet reinforcement column was destroyed by *I./SS-Pz.Rgt.3*. At 11:00 Jeremejewka finally fell into the hands

SS grenadiers watching a hurricane of fire unleashed by *Newbelwerfer* batteries of the *SS-Panzer-Korps*, 1943.

A German artillery position on the Ukrainian front, 1943.

of the SS troops. *Panzergruppe Meierdress* cut to shreds an enemy group fleeing towards Jefremowka. At Sofjewka, the *15.Kp./'T'* captured more than three hundred Soviet soldiers and destroyed numerous *T-34* tanks and armored cars. At 12:40, the *Totenkopf* intercepted a Soviet regiment in the Dmitrowka area. Against it the division sent elements of the logistics train and of *SS-Pz.Rgt.3*. Fighting against that regiment continued throughout the day and was resolved the following day with the complete destruction of the Soviet unit.

A *PzKpfw III* of *SS-Pz.Rgt.3* in the Jeremejewka sector. (NARA)

SS-Hstuf. Erwin Meierdress.

Around 15:00, contact was made with *Leibstandarte* troops at Jeremejewka. But at around 16:00, the *Eicke* Regiment reported that due to the poor state of the roads it could not continue its attack: ammunition resupply had for the time being been halted. With that the possibility of wiping out the Soviet units north of Jeremejewka vanished. In the Pawlowka sector, the forward outposts of *SS-Aufkl.-Abt. 'T'* spotted a Soviet cavalry unit in the valley of the Bogotaja River. Before the alarm could be given the Soviet horsemen, with their sabers unsheathed, attacked the German positions, making their way through the village without losing a single man. An artillery observer, more alert than the recon troops, began to call in artillery fire on the cavalrymen who were charging in the valley. It was a veritable massacre. Only a few survivors managed to disappear to the east. At the end of the day, the *Totenkopf* reported that it had knocked out twenty-four enemy tanks. At that point, the Soviet 3rd Tank Army could be considered to have been completely destroyed. During the night between March 3-4, the Soviets once again attempted to escape from the pocket. They were met by elements of the division's logistics train.

March 1: Troops of *I.(gep)./SS-Pz.Gr.Rgt.1 'T'* entering Oleniki. (NARA)

A *PzKpfw III* of the *Totenkopf* entering into a village.

Seeking refuge in small villages in the area to escape from the SS troops, these isolated Soviet groups caused problems for the *SS-Pz.Korps* supply organization. Throughout the day, the *Totenkopf* continued sweeps inside the pocket. Around noontime, the *SS-Pz.Korps* ordered Max Simon to speed up the elimination of Soviet troops remaining in the pocket so that the division could resume its offensive against Kharkov. Lacking the necessary experience to lead an armored division, Max Simon had in fact made the mistake of parceling out his panzers to various *Kampfgruppen* in order to deal with the Soviet infiltrations rather than concentrating them to prosecute the attack to the north. Based on orders he had received, *SS-Brigdf.* Simon then organized a strong *Kampfgruppe* with *I.(gep.)/SS-Pz.Gren.Rgt.1 'T'*, *I./SS-Art.-Rgt.3*, elements of *I./SS-Pz.Gren.Rgt.3 'TE'*, a *Flak* battery and an assault gun battery. This combat group, commanded by *SS-Hstuf.* Reder, left Jeremejewka to move towards the pocket, where it wiped out numerous enemy columns. In the evening, Reder reported that he had destroyed or captured 13 tanks, 11 armored cars, 82 artillery pieces and anti-tank guns and more than 300 vehicles. On the plain at Jeremjewka, the German victory was key to the prosecution of operations: more than three thousand Soviet soldiers had been killed, 36 tanks, 11 armored cars, 159 guns, 520 trucks and 352 other vehicles had been destroyed or captured by the *Totenkopf*.

One of the assault guns supporting the *16.(Pi.)Kp./SS-Pz.Rgt.3*, during the attack on Mariewka.

A group of SS grenadiers with an *MG-42* machine gun.

The number of its own tanks available, however, had fallen to 81 vehicles: 41 *PzKpfw.II*, 11 *PzKpfw IV*, 6 *Bef.Pz.*, 6 *PzKpfw VI Tiger* and 17 *StuG III*. It should be noted that in the early morning, the *11.Panzerdivision* (*XLVIII.Korps*) had reached the banks of the Orel and had made contact with *SS-Pi.-Btl.3* south of Jefremowka. In addition to the destruction of the 3rd Tank Army, the Germans had caused the 6th Army and the 1st Guards Army to withdraw, while units of *4.Panzerarmee* were advancing in force towards Kharkov. In the *Korps z.b.V Raus* sector, the Soviet 69th Army, surprised by the German counteroffensive, also began to pull back its divisions.

A column of assault guns on the move in the Jeremejewka sector.

The attack continues

On March 5, the *SS-Pz.Korps* was engaged in eliminating Soviet forces south of the Msha River, between Walki and Baschmetjewka, in preparation for the offensive towards Khakov. During the night between 6 and 7 March, the *Eicke* Regiment took positions on the left flank of the *SS-Pz.Korps* in the sector situated to the west of Walki, traveling along a road that was congested with vehicles of the *Leibstandarte* and transformed into a morass by the intense traffic and the thaw. The sector also had to be cleared of the last pockets of enemy resistance. In particular, the *II./'T'* had to fight strenuously to eliminate Soviet troops who had holed up in the Kawanzewka school buildings. A Soviet shell exploded

Das Reich motorcycle scouts.

right in the middle of the battalion headquarters and wounded its commander, *SS-Stubaf.* Schulze. Unit command then passed to *SS-Hstuf.* Eckert. Meanwhile, *Korps z.b.V. Raus* had been ordered to cut off the retreat of the 3rd Tank Army and to protect the left flank of the *SS-Pz.Korps*. Just at that moment, the Soviets were shifting a number of rifle divisions of the 69th Army towards the Msha River sector. At 5:00, the *Thule* regiment kicked off an attack in support of the *Grossdeutschland*, moving from Stepanowka, with the aim of recapturing Iskrowka and Shelestowo. After having crossed through a dense forest, the grenadiers of *I./Thule* ended up in a partisan training camp. *SS-Stubaf.* Häussler left one of his companies on the spot and directed the bulk of his battalion against Iskrowka. Having gotten to within about eight hundred meters south of the village, however, the SS troops were stalled by a solid defensive system and came under enemy fire. The enemy bunkers had to be cleaned out one after another. Once the Soviet resistance was overcome, Häussler regrouped his battalion south of Shelestowo and prepared to support the attack of *Gruppe Wätjen* of the *Grossdeutschland* with the tanks of *Panzerzug 62*. The Soviets were well dug in southeast of that location, along an high elevated

A *Totenkopf* artillery detachment emplacing a gun in a Ukrainian village, March 1943. (NARA)

A Blocking position with a heavy *MG-34* to close the pocket.

embankment. The *3.Kp./Thule*, the *2.Bttr./SS-StuG.-Abt.3* and the *Grossdeutschland* scouts hit the Soviets in the flank and invested the village. They had to fight street by street and house by house. Soviet resistance proved to be very tenacious so it was decided to bypass the position and continue to move forward.

Assault guns and SPW of *Kampfgruppe Reder* engaged in wiping out the last nests of resistance in the Jeremejewka pocket, March 1943. (NARA)

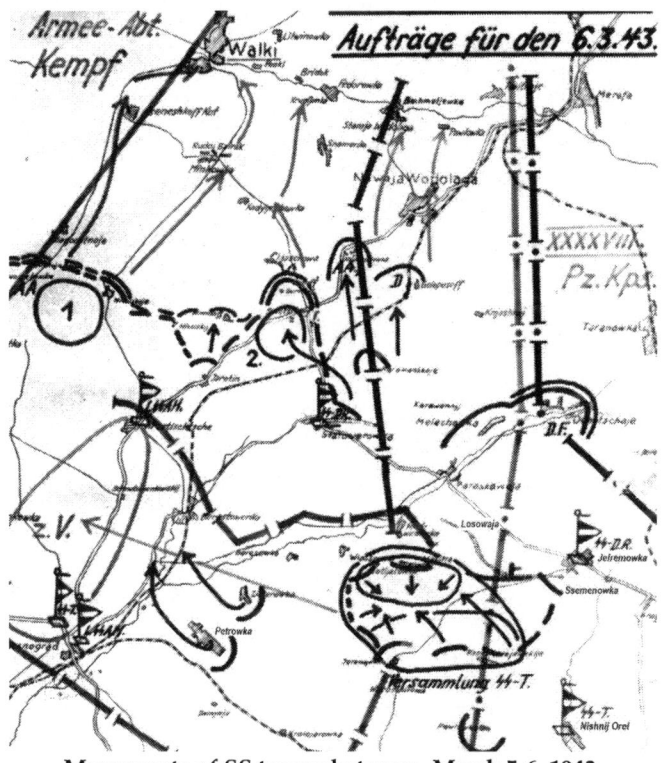

Movements of SS troops between March 5-6, 1943.

Assault against Kharkov

On March 8, the *SS-Pz.Korps* continued its offensive aimed at encircling Kharkov from the west. The bulk of the *Das Reich* pushed on past Odrinka, while the *Leibstandarte* took Staryi Ljubotin. Reports indicated that the Soviets were no longer fighting with their usual stubbornness. On the other hand, further to the east, the *XLVIII.Pz.Korps* and the *LVII.Pz.Korps* ran up against extremely strong and determined resistance. Meanwhile, after the sudden thaw of the previous days, the cold returned and snowstorms significantly limited visibility. In the morning, the Totenkopf continued its sweeps of the sector to the south of Walki. The *Eicke* Regiment seized Staryi Mertschik at 17:00 and later linked up with units of *Panzergruppe von Strachwitz* (armored elements of *Grossdeutschland*) near Walki. The *Totenkopf* troops now had to encircle Kharkov from the north.

To that purpose, *SS-Kampfgruppe Baum*, consisting of the *Totenkopf* Regiment, the *SS-Aufkl.-Abt. 'T'* and a few assault guns, moved in early evening to Schljach, a railway station situated on the Kowjagi-Ljubotin-Kharkov line.

A German assault gun on the Ukrainian front, March 1943. (NARA)

Waffen-SS half-tracks and *StuG* during a halt.

The following day the *Totenkopf* troops were to capture Olschany, a city situated northwest of Kharkov, then to turn east, cutting the roads that led to Kharkov from the north. Meanwhile, *Das Reich* was to break through the Soviet defenses southwest of Kharkov and push to the east to support the attack of *XLVIII.Pz.Korps*. That corps was supposed to push to the southeast of Kharkov to cut off the Soviet escape route. During the night between 8 and 9 March, *SS-Kampfgruppe Baum* attacked and invested Olschany at 4:00. That important road and rail hub was found strangely free of enemy forces. The SS combat group then continued on towards the Udy area, establishing bridgeheads near the station at Peressetschnaja, at Jarotawka and at Golowaschtschew.

A group of SS grenadiers moving to attack, supported by an MG-34.

Grossdeutschland soldiers.

Subsequently, *Totenkopf* troops made contact with *SS-Kampfgruppe Witt* of the *Leibstandarte* to the north of Peressetschnaja. In the afternoon, the *I.(gep.)/'T'* pushed even further north and seized Tschepelin. During the fighting its commander, *SS-Hstuf.* Reder, was gravely wounded: shell splinters wounded his left arm, his right hand and his throat. Transferred to a field hospital, the next day, due to the serious wounds he had sustained, his left forearm was amputated. Lacking its commander, the battalion dug into defensive positions.

Around 12:00, when the *Leibstandarte*, the *Das Reich* and the *Totenkopf* attacked west and southwest of Kharkov, the *4.Panzerarmee* asked the *SS-Pz.Korps* via radio if Kharkov could be seized by a swift attack. Hausser's answer was clear: *"A swift attack at best, possible for 10 March"*. To better explain the exact intention of that *"strange"* communication, Hausser then reminded the *4.Panzerarmee* that such

Movement of the three SS divisions towards Kharkov.

SS grenadiers attacking an enemy position.

an operation did not enter within the parameters of the mission assigned to his army corps! At 17:05, not having received any further orders for the following day, Hausser decided to capture Kharkov: the *Leibstandarte* was to attack from the north, the *Das Reich* from the west and the *Totenkopf* was to remain as a covering force to block any Soviet counterattacks coming from the north or northwest. To reinforce the *Das Reich*, the *Totenkopf* was to put a tactical group at its disposition, commanded by *SS-Stubaf.* Kunstmann and consisting of *II./SS-Pz.Rgt.3* (minus the *Tiger-Kompanie*) and the *II./'T'*; the group began its march during the night between 9 and 10 March. Around 20:00, *4.Panzerarmee* ended up revealing its intentions: on March 10, the *SS-Pz.Korps* was to reach the Lopan area, between Kharkov and Dergatschi and then close in on Kharkov from the west and from the north. Thus all of the conditions could be put in place to capture the city with a swift attack. In addition, on March 10, at 19:00, *Heeresgruppe Süd* sent a telex to *4.Panzerarmee* and to *Armee-Abteilung Kempf* which clearly mentioned the possibility of seizing Kharkov in case Soviet resistance had weakened significantly. The center of gravity of the *SS-Pz.Korps* offensive thus shifted to its left flank, with the *Leibstandarte* and the *Totenkopf* which were to attack to the northeast in order to take Kharkov from the north. On March 10, around 7:00, *SS-Kampfgruppe Baum*, supported by the *Tiger-Kompanie* under *SS-Hstuf.* Richter, went on the attack, moving from Golowaschtschewka. The heavy Tiger tanks destroyed the Soviet anti-tank guns one after another. Around 13:00, the *Kampfgruppe* seized the northern neighborhoods of Dergatschi; the town was also attacked by tanks from the *Leibstandarte*. The Soviets fled to the northeast. This allowed the *Leibstandarte* to move to the south, towards Kharkov.

In front of a *PzKpfw III* of the *Totenkopf*, last-minute details of the action to circle Kharkov from the north are discussed: recognizable on the left is *SS-Hstuf.* Meyer and in front of the *Panzer III* is *SS-Stubaf.* Kunstmann, commander of *II./SS-Pz.Rgt.3*.

Grenadiers of the *SS-Pz.Korps* on the march towards Kharkov.

Soviet resistance intensified on the outskirts of the large Ukrainian city. In the afternoon, *SS-Kampfgruppe Baum* attacked to the east, just to the north of the *SS-Kampfgruppe Witt* route of march. At 15:00 it reached Tscherkaskaja Losowaja, where it turned northeast. At 16:00, the *15.Kp./'T'* took Russkaja Losowaja with a bold attack. The road to Kharkov was thus secured, which was very important, because it was one of the rare roads in the region that could handle traffic reliably. In the late afternoon of that same day, *SS-Pz.Rgt.3* had 30 *PzKpfw III*, 14 *PzKpfw IV* and 5 *PzKpfw VI* still operational. During the evening of March 10, the *SS-Pz.Korps* was ready to move on Kharkov. At dawn on the following day, March 11, troops of the *Leibstandarte* moved into the northern suburbs of Kharkov; Fritz Witt's regiment managed to get as far as the city's Red Square. The fleeing Soviets then attempted to pass through the positions held by *Totenkopf* troops.

A *StuG III* near an artillery emplacement.

A *Tiger* tank in defilade behind a house during an attack.

An *SdKfz.251* of *SS-Kampfgruppe Baum* inside Dergatschi.

At Solotschew, *SS-Pz.Jg.-Abt.3* staved off two enemy attacks and the *Eicke* Regiment wiped out a Soviet formation at Rogosjanka. In the afternoon the *4.Panzerarmee* ordered the *SS-Pz.Korps* to regroup: the *Das Reich* was to relieve the *Totenkopf* north of Kharkov, because the division was to prevent the escape of Soviet units to the east and had to detach a *Kampfgruppe* to send to Tschugujew. This order stemmed from the failure of the *XLVIII.Pz.Korps* attack south of the Msha River. Paul Hausser protested against this change of objective, just when his forces were in the middle of an offensive: considering the situation and the condition of the roads, *SS-Ogruf.* Paul Hausser estimated that it would take at least a day and a half for the *Das Reich* to relieve the *Totenkopf* troops north of Kharkov. He thus intended to prosecute the attack as planned and to regroup his divisions only after having captured Kharkov. Nevertheless, the *Totenkopf* organized a new *SS-Kampfgruppe Baum*, based on the *Totenkopf* Regiment. On the front of *Armee-Abteilung Kempf*, engaged in pushing the troops of the Soviet 40th and 69th armies from Kharkov, the *Thule* Regiment took Krasnokutsk and Murafa, while troops of the *Grossdeutschland* division were busy seizing Bogoduchow. On March 12, the *4.Panzerarmee* confirmed the order to attack towards Tschugejew to prevent the Soviets from escaping to the east.

That mission was assigned to the *Totenkopf* and to the *Das Reich*, but *Das Reich* could not yet disengage because its troops were still committed against strong enemy forces in the center of the city. The *SS-Pz.Korps* then ordered it to open a passage through Kharkov. *SS-Kampfgruppe Kunstmann*, consisting mainly of II./SS-Pz.Rgt.3 under *SS-Hstuf.* Kunstmann, was also ordered to disengage and to regroup north of Kharkov towards evening. From there it then headed towards the tractor factory, passing through Bol.Danilowka. *SS-Kampfgruppe Baum* instead attempted to move to the southeast, towards Tschugujew. In an attempt to stop the movement of German troops, the Soviets brought in fresh armored formations, some of which, around noontime, overran the *Totenkopf* forward outposts at Bairak and continued on towards Bol.Danilowka; *Stukas* from *Luftflotte 4* intervened to hit them from the air, upon request of the *SS-Pz.Korps*. Numerous Soviet tanks and artillery pieces were thus destroyed. *SS-Kampfgruppe Baum* took advantage of the opportunity to retake the position at Bairak and to put up a defensive perimeter. The rest of the *Totenkopf* troops set up a series of strongpoints along a line that ran through Russkaja Losowaja, Sotniki, Dolshik and Rogosjanka. A few hours later, other Soviet troops launched fresh attacks supported by tanks, managing to recapture Zirkuny. Even before the enemy could consolidate his positions, around 14:00, the *I./'TE'* counterattacked and reclaimed the town following

Tanks of *Kampfgruppe Kunstmann*, stalled in front of an anti-tank ditch on the western outskirts of Kharkov.

Grenadiers of the *II./1 'T'* on board a *PzKpfw.IV* of 7./SS-Pz.Rgt.3. (NARA)

furious close-quarter fighting in the streets and houses. Meanwhile, in the *Korps z.b.V. Raus* sector, the *Thule* Regiment was relieved by troops from the *167.Infanterie-Division* and reached the Olschany sector, where they again came under *Totenkopf* control.

Elements of *SS-StuG.-Abt. 'T'* north of Kharkov. (NARA)

Grenadiers and tanks of *Kampfgruppe Kunstmann*.

PzKpfw.IV. 712 of 7./Kp./SS-Pz.Rgt.3 at Kharkov. (NARA)

The march to Rogan

During the night between the 12th and 13th, the *Totenkopf* began to regroup its forces. The majority of the units that had been left in defensive positions north of Kharkov were relieved and sent to support *SS-Kampfgruppe Baum*. Baum's troops continued their advance towards Rogan as day broke, running into considerable difficulties, because of the lack of roads that ran from west to east as well as due to the obstinate resistance by the Soviets. Once some enemy positions had been overcome, *SS-Kampfgruppe Baum* continued its advance towards the Kharkov-Tschugujew road. On its right, *SS-Kampfgruppe Harmel* of the *2.SS-Pz.Div. Das Reich* was fighting, which had come to reinforce *SS-Kampfgruppe Kunstmann*.

A *Totenkopf Pz.IV* inside Kharkov.

The *Pz.IV* of *SS-Ostuf.* **Hans Behr, commander of** *7./Kp./SS-Pz.Rgt.3,* **entering into Kharkov.**

Grenadiers and *Panzers* of the *Totenkopf* on the march towards Rogan.

At 15:00, Otto Baum's men arrived on the hills located north of Rogan. The Soviets then mounted a counterattack using tanks and infantry units. The *Totenkopf* tanks engaged them at long range, exploiting the superiority of their optical systems and the range of their guns; about a dozen *T-34* tanks were thus quickly destroyed. The fighting lasted for hours. Stalled by the German fire, the Soviets dug in around the tractor factory. At nightfall, *SS-Kampfgruppe Baum* entered the city and made contact with *SS-Kampfgruppe Harmel* north of the tractor factory. In the evening, the *SS-Pz.Korps* announced that two-thirds of Kharkov was in its hands. At that time, the *Totenkopf* held the line Russkaja Losowaja, Russkije Tischky, Zirkuny,Sorokowa and Rogan. Otto Baum's troops resumed the attack towards Tschugujew on the morning of 14 March. At 11:00 they reached the hills in the area to the east of Rogan, where they were halted for three hours because of lack of fuel. In the afternoon the SS troops resumed their march after having been resupplied by air; having reached the position in front of Kamennaja Jaruga, they clashed with troops of the 3rd Guards Rifle Division, which had recently arrived in that sector. The battle was bitter and fighting was from house to house. The devastating German firepower again made the difference. With air support from the Stukas, enemy strongpoints were reduced to silcence one after another and the position was taken by SS troops during the night. The Soviets left many dead on the field and a great amount of material in German hands. At that point only one bridge separated the men of *SS-*

Kampfgruppe Baum from Tschgujew. On the same day of March 14, 1943, German radio interrupted its normal programming and over the notes of the Horst Wessel Lied announced that *"Waffen SS units, with the support of the Luftwaffe, after days of fierce combat and an encircling attack from the north and east, have recaptured Kharkov"*.

Elements of *Kampfgruppe Kunstmann* in the streets of Kharkov: grenadiers of II./1 'T' and PzKpfw IV of 7./Kp./SS-Pz.Rgt.3.

SS-Ostubaf. Otto Baum.

The attack towards Tsuguschew

During the night between March 14-15, the *III./'T'* launched its attack towards Tsuguschew. The *I.(gep.)/'T'* entered the city from the southwest. At 9:48 Tsuguschew was firmly in the hands of the SS troops; the encirclement of Kharkov was now complete. The *Totenkopf* now had to extend its right wing as far as the Udy River and make contact with the *6.Pz.Div*. This would allow the complete destruction of the forces that remained trapped between the *SS-Pz.Korps* and the *XLVIII.Pz.Korps*. At that time the *Totenkopf* had only twenty-five tanks and eight assault guns still operational. The SS troops now had to continue on to the Donetz, more precisely, towards Woltschansk, in order to establish defensive positions. The three divisions of the corps had to attack side by side to the north, with the *Totenkopf* in the Tschugujew-Werchnij

Salkow sector. On March 16, two problems cropped up that the *SS-Pz.Korps* had to resolve: west of the Tschugujew-Rogan-Bairak blocking line, the encircled Soviet forces were much larger than had been thought and were trying to flee to the northeast. The German "pincers" did not seem to be strong enough to contain them.

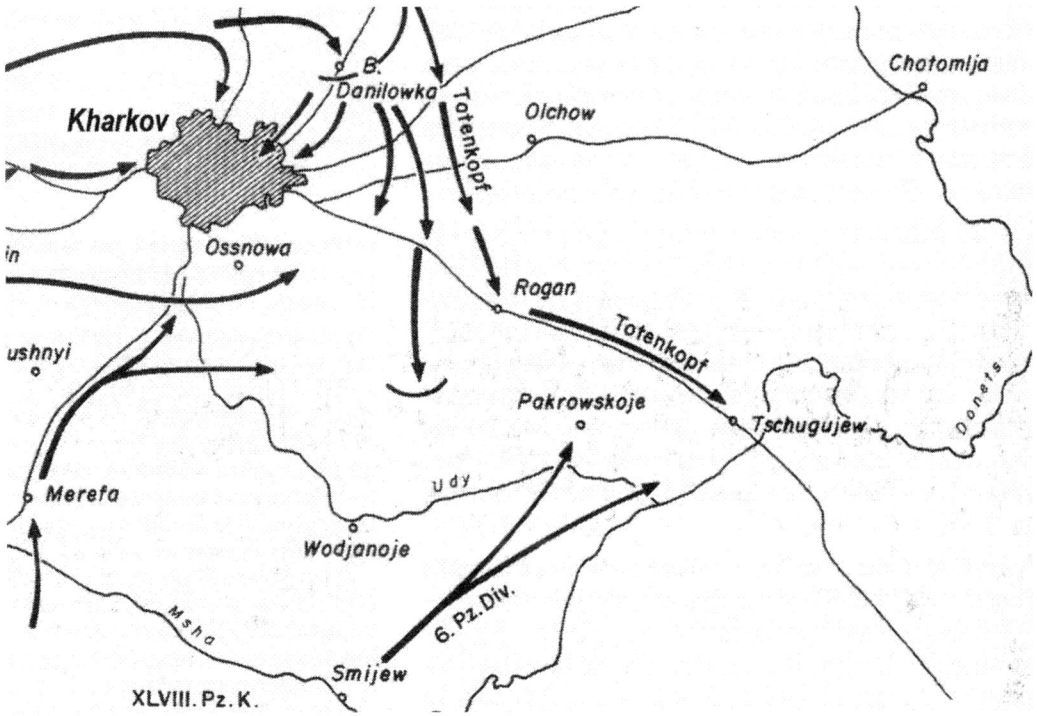

Totenkopf movements in the area east of Kharkov, March 1943.

SS-Hstuf. Waldemar Riefkogel.

In addition, the Soviets were preparing a counterattack along the Woltschansk-Kharkov road with reinforcements that had arrived from Bjelgorod. In particular, the *Totenkopf* positions were attacked throughout the day by Soviet units attempting to escape from the encirclement. All of those attacks were warded off, but the division was nailed to the spot for the whole day. In the critical city of Tschugujew the Soviets were able to recapture the northern part of the city. They were pushed out again during the night, due mainly to the efforts of the *10.Kp./'T'*. In the meantime, southwest of the city, strong Soviet forces, exploiting their numerical superiority, eliminated the German outposts and made haste to attack the city again. It was then that three tanks of the *3.Kp./SSPz.Rgt.3* under *SS-Ostuf.* Waldemar Riefkogel joined the action. Their sudden appearance caused panic among the Soviet infantry, who began to run in all directions. Two *T-34* tanks were knocked out during this fighting. A second Soviet attack was driven off soon after, under similar conditions, but around 17:00 a fresh dense mass of Soviet infantry threw itself against the positions defended by the SS troops. These were rapidly overrun: *SS-Ostuf*. Riefkogel again came to the rescue.

SS grenadiers on the snow-covered steppe of the Donetz, March 1943.

A German armored formation in an attack.

The *T-34* tanks accompanying the infantry were knocked out, following which the SS panzers charged against the enemy infantry, who withdrew in great disorder. The southern part of the city once again fell into the hands of the SS troops. At the end of the day, faced with this new situation, *4.Panzerarmee* changed its plans: the principal objective was no longer Woltschansk, but was now Bjelgorod. At 9:10 on March 17, *Kampfgruppe Oppeln* of the *6.Panzerdivision* reached the area southeast of Tschugujew, where it made contact with *Kampfgruppe Baum*. Thus reinforced by the panzers, that combat group began to clean out the city, neighborhood by neighborhood. Fighting flared up mainly in the southern area, along the railway line, then to the north of Tschugujew where the Soviets had many tanks hidden amongst the ruined buildings. At the conclusion of the battle, the Germans claimed the destruction of twenty-one *T-34* and *T-70* tanks, but *Totenkopf* losses were also high. Tschugujew was finally cleared by the SS troops during the afternoon.

A *PzKpfw IV* of 3./SS-Pz.Rgt.3 supporting the grenadiers, March 1943.

An *SdKfz.250* armed with an *MG-34*, March 1943.

Soon after, the *Totenkopf* troops were pulled back from the front near Sarosknoje in anticipation of their transfer to the region southwest of Nepokrytaja to attack towards Bjelgorod. Following the capture of Sarosknoje, the Totenkopf was to prepare to follow the attack of the other two divisions of the *SS-Panzerkorps*. The *schwere Kompanie* was committed with four Tigers near Bolschaja Babka.

Bibliography
M. Afiero, "*Totenkopf*", Marvia Edizioni
M. Afiero, "*3.SS-Pz.Div. Totenkopf - Vol. I: 1939-1943*", Associazione Culturale Ritterkreuz
M. Afiero, "*The 3rd Waffen-SS Pz.Div. Totenkopf 1939-1943: Vol.1*", Schiffer Publishing

SS-Unterscharführer Egon Christophersen
by Antonio Guerra

Egon Christophersen, *Unterscharführer* in the *Waffen-SS* during World War II, was the first of three Danish volunteers to be decorated with the Knight's Cross of the Iron Cross. He was born on February 8, 1919 in Strøby in Denmark. From the age of seven he started attending the local school in Strøby and then worked on an experimental farm from the age of fourteen with his three brothers. With the onset of war, Christophersen joined the National Socialist Workers' Party of Denmark, shortly after becoming a member of its armed militia, the *Storm Afdeling*. On April 7, 1941, he enlisted in the *Waffen-SS*. He was then transferred to Graz to complete his basic training with the reserve battalion of the *SS-Regiment Der Führer*. After completing his training, he was assigned to 11.*Kompanie* of *SS-Regiment Nordland* of *SS-Division Wiking* in August 1941, but was soon transferred to 9.*Kp./Nordland*. When the division was transferred to the Eastern Front, Christophersen was again transferred to another company, this time 2.*Kp./Nordland*.

SS-*Unterscharführer* **Egon Christophersen**

Christophersen (left) on leave in Denmark.

In May 1942, he was promoted to *Sturmmann*. During the fighting in the Caucasus, he was wounded in both thighs and was evacuated to a military hospital in September 1942. After his recovery, he was transferred to the depot battalion of the *SS-Regiment Westland* in Graz. Christophersen remained in Graz until February 1943, when he returned to his division, the *Wiking*, meanwhile transformed into a new division of armored grenadiers. He was decorated with the Iron Cross Second Class for outstanding combat in the Caucasus and was promoted to *Unterscharführer*.

A *Danmark* motorized column on the move in Croatia, Spring 1943 (NARA).

***Danmark* soldiers in a defensive position in Croatia.**

In May 1943, Christophersen was transferred to the newly formed SS Division *Nordland*, formed around the SS-Regiment *Norland*, quartered at Grafenwohr. He was then assigned to the *7.Kompanie* of the new *SS-Panzergrenadier Regiment 24 'Danmark'*, composed mainly of Danish volunteers. After completing the training, this unit was sent to Croatia to be engaged against the Tito partisan formations. Egon's brother Viggo, also enlisted in the *Waffen-SS*, was killed around this time. The SS-Division *Nordland* together with the SS *Nederland* Brigade, united in the *III.(Germ.)SS-Panzer-Korps*, were transferred between December 1943 and January 1944 to the Leningrad front, in the Oranienbaum sector.

On the Narva front

After the retreat from the Leningrad front, the units of the III.(Germ.)SS-Pz.Korps stood on the Narva front since February 1944. The defensive fighting lasted for months, until spring and the beginning of summer. Christophersen's 7.Kp./Danmark was entrenched in the area south of Narva and east of Kreenholm, next to the Dolgaya Niva district. These positions were attacked by Soviet units as early as May 20 and in the following days. On June 7, 1944, the Soviets launched an attack against the outpost of Sonnenschein defended by 7./Danmark, causing numerous losses among the Danish volunteers. The remnants of the company, under the command of the SS-Ustuf. Danish Leo Madsen, somehow managed to repel this first attack. Five days later, the Soviets attacked again, preceded by a heavy bombardment from their artillery. The Sonnenschein sector thus found itself completely isolated. Soviet artillerymen used smoke shells that covered the whole landscape under an artificial fog. The clouds of smoke also reached the II./Danmark

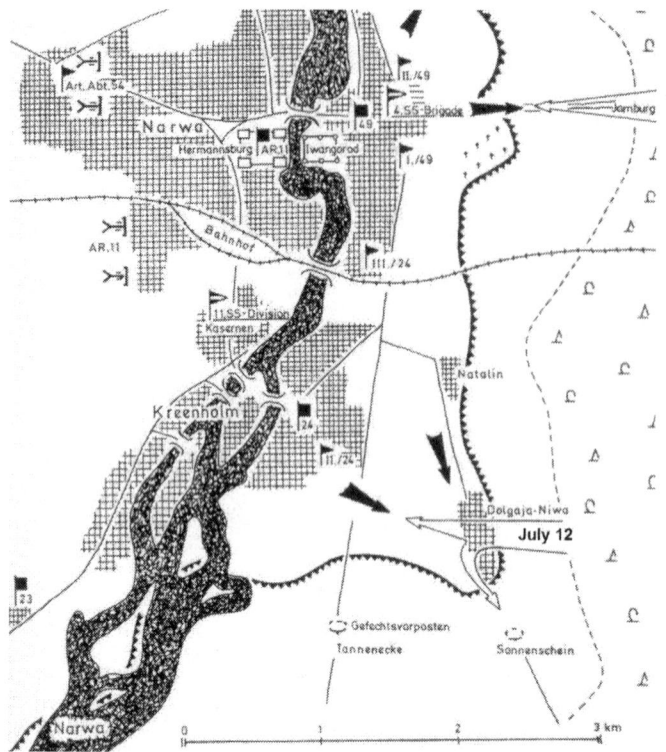

Deployment of German forces on the Narva bridgehead. Below right, the positions of *Danmark* with the outpost of Sonnenschein.

Danmark grenadiers in a trench, 1944.

command post at Dolgaja-Niva. A few minutes later, *SS-Ustuf*. Madsen fired a flare to call for help, as the remnants of his company were totally surrounded at Sonnenschein. He knew very well that he could not hold the position for long, so he decided to attempt a breakthrough maneuver to reach his battalion at Dolgaja-Niva. But by then it was too late, the Soviet grip was firmly tightened around them. Under the cover of fog and the roar of explosions, Soviet soldiers again attacked the positions of *7./Danmark*, triggering fierce hand-to-hand combat. Two platoon commanders fell at the head of their men, *SS-Ustuf.* Johannes Koopmann and *SS-Ustuf.* Arne Michaelsen.

A *Nordland* machine-gun squad in an advanced position on the Narva front, Summer 1944.

Danmark **Grenadiers before an attack, Summer 1944.**

Only a group of about ten men, led by *SS-Uscha.* Egon Christophersen, continued to hold out, on the north wing of the position. The rocket fired by Madsen at the start of the attack had been seen from the observation post of the *Nordland* Artillery Regiment. The guns swung into action and sent a deluge of fire into the area east of Dolgaja-Niva, where the Soviets had massed their troops. Meanwhile, at least two hundred Soviet infantry had already charged through the breach and managed to gain more ground. Other Soviet units came out of the forests and charged into the already under attack position. The guns of *SS-Ostubaf.* Karl adjusted their fire well, literally pulverizing the Soviet infantry, who disappeared amid smoke and explosions. But other enemy forces arrived soon after and it seemed that nothing could stop the Soviet units, which continued to attack, despite the heavy losses suffered: the Soviets now seemed to be masters of the Sonnenschein outpost and were also pushing into Dolgaja-Niva, where it was house to house fighting.

Danmark **Grenadiers fighting on the Narva beachhead, Summer 1944.**

Danmark **grenadiers in a trench, Summer 1944.**

The group led by Christophersen, still held, despite being totally surrounded. Norwegian *SS-Hstuf.* Erik Lärum, commander of *13./Danmark*, equipped with 150mm howitzers, had observed the fighting around Sonnenschein from his forward position and seeing the seriousness of the situation, he decided to temporarily abandon his howitzers, to help the SS grenadiers.

By placing himself at the head of a combat group, including his gunners and the grenadiers of the two heavy companies of the *II.* and *III./Danmark*, Lärum counterattacked. In addition, Lärum requested mortar and artillery support from the divisional command: all guns and heavy weapons in the sector concentrated their fire on the Soviet positions around Dolgaja-Niva. Completely engulfed in a firestorm, Soviet soldiers were forced to seek cover to avoid being killed.

Radio operator from regiment *Danmark*, 1944.

***SS-Uscha.* from Regiment *Danmark*.**

A wounded kamerad on Narwa front, Summer 1944.

Soon after the artillery action, a counter-attack was launched with all available forces: *SS-Hstuf.* Herbert Meyer arrived with part of his *9./Danmark* to participate in the assault against Dolgaja-Niva, while other elements of *8.* and *16./Danmark* arrived as reinforcements along with two *StuG III* assault guns. The *Danmark* grenadiers arrived shortly after among the trenches where the survivors of the Soviet attack had taken refuge, took about forty prisoners and reconquered the lost ground. Soon after, the link was established with their comrades of the *7.Kompanie*, grouped around *SS-Uscha.* Christophersen. The Danish sergeant had not waited for reinforcements to arrive, to launch counterattacks with his handful of grenadiers south and north of his position, thus managing to break the encirclement.

SS-Uscha. Christophersen with EK I.

SS-Uscha. Christophersen with *Ritterkreuz*.

SS-Uscha. Christophersen

SS-Hstuf. Heinz Hämel, who had gone to the front line, joined the Danish non-commissioned officer, whom he knew very well, when he had been in command of his company, to personally decorate him with the Iron Cross First Class and subsequently recommend him for the Knight's Cross, the first Danish volunteer to receive it, which was officially granted to him on 11 July 1944. Only three Danes were awarded the Knight's Cross during WWII, the other two being *SS-Ostuf.* Søren Kam and *SS-Ostuf.* Johannes Hellmers. Egon Christophersen survived the war and returned to live in Køge in Denmark. He worked in Ørum in the Hansen factory for over thirty years. He died on January 15, 1988.

Bibliography

Massimiliano Afiero, "11.SS-Freiwilligen-Panzergrenadier-Division Nordland", Ass. Cult. Ritterkreuz

Walther-Peer Fellgiebel, "*Elite of the Third Reich, The recipients of the Knight's Cross of the Iron Cross 1939-1945: A Reference*", Helion & Company Limited

Walther-Peer Fellgiebel, "*Die Träger des Ritterkreuzes des Eisernen Kreuzes 1939-1945*", Podzun-Pallas

Veit Scherzer, "*Ritterkreuzträger 1939 - 1945 Die Inhaber des Ritterkreuzes des Eisernen Kreuzes 1939 von Heer, Luftwaffe, Kriegsmarine, Waffen-SS, ...*", Scherzers Miltaer-Verlag.

The Tunisian campaign
By Massimiliano and Ralph Riccio

Almost concurrent with the final battle at El Alamein, on 7 November the Allies launched Operation *'Torch'*, consisting of the landing of 70,000 American and British troops at Casablanca, Oran and Algiers in French North Africa. The Axis reaction to the landings was to send motorized forces to Tunisia to cover the retreat of the forces in Libya and to challenge the Anglo-American advance from the French colonies. In early November, the first Italian units to land in Tunisia were 10th Bersaglieri Regiment, one airborne battalion, the DLVII 75/18 SP group, and the CI and CXXXVI L40 antitank battalions. The Germans sent an airborne regiment, several infantry battalions and advance elements of *10.Panzer-Division*. These reinforcements attempted to expand the bridgehead in Tunisia and to establish contact with the troops retreating from Libya as well as rebuffing Anglo-American attempts to prevent that linkup. The *'Centauro'* armored division, which had also arrived in early November, ceded its XV Battalion to the *'Superga'* infantry division and then to the 50th Special Brigade. The XIV and XVII tank battalions and the lone company of the XVI Battalion which reached North

General Giovanni Messe, commander of the Italian 1st Army in Tunisia. Messe had previously served as commander of all Italian forces in Russia and is considered by many historians to have been the best Italian general of the Second World War.

German Panzer entering outskirts of a Tunisian village.

Africa had been assigned to the *Raggruppamento Cantaluppi*, which included what was left of *'Ariete'* and which, in early 1943 was redesignated as the *'Centauro'* armored division, reinforced with the 7th Bersaglieri Regiment, the *'Lodi'* reconnaissance detachment and the *'Volpi'* artillery raggruppamento. Some of the tank companies had been equipped with 75/18 SP guns in lieu of M14 tanks.

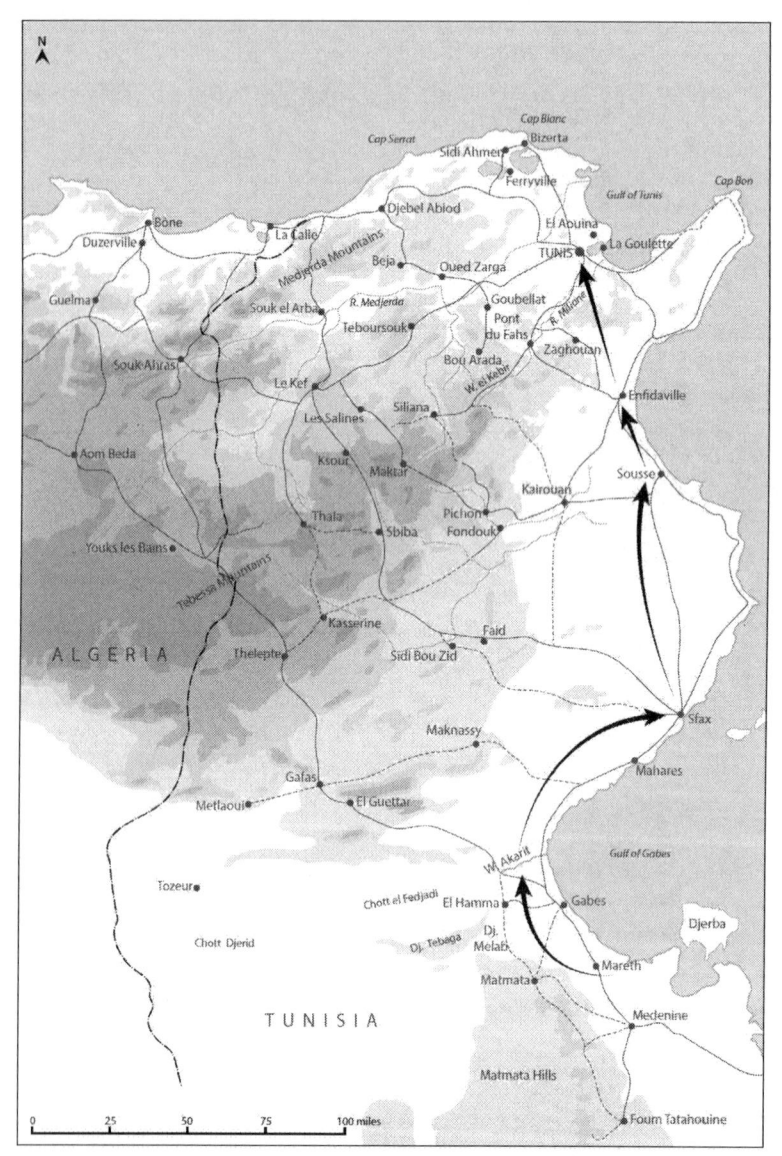

Eighth Army advance into Tunisia, December 1942 - May 1943.

On 11 November the advance elements of the 1st Infantry Divison (Mountain) *'Superga'* disembarked at Bizerte, Tunisia, reflecting the urgency on the part of Comando Supremo to attempt to salvage the situation in North Africa. The division's commander, General Dante Lorenzelli, who had landed by air, quickly established battle groups and established defensive positions at Mateur, Sidi bou Zid and Sidi Belkai.

On 14 November the *'Centauro'* division's XV Battalion, which had been attached to *'Superga'*, fought off a US formation at Sened, knocking out 24 tanks and capturing a number of prisoners. The Italian units that had just arrived in North Africa successfully fought on the night of 24 November blocking – along with other Italo-German units – a strong British attack south of Mateur, losing three SP guns.

A pair of M13/40 tanks on a reconnaissance mission in late 1942. (USSME)

Generaloberst **Hans-Jürgen von Arnim (Left).**

On 22 November a tank detachment from Italian 50th Special Brigade heading from Gabes to Gafsa was ambushed by US paratroopers who knocked out five M14s. The 50th Special Brigade (frequently referred to as the *'Imperiali'* Brigade after the name of its commander, General Giovanni Imperiali di Francavilla) consisted of the 6th Infantry Battalion, the DLVII self-propelled 75/18 group, and the XV Tank Battalion from *'Centauro'*. On 26 November during a raid against Gafsa the US paratroopers again tangled with the XV Battalion, but were driven off after having destroyed a fuel dump. On 10 December the Italians occupied El Guettar and Maknassy, establishing solid defensive positions there. On 24 January 1943 the US 1st Armored

Division engaged elements of the 50th Brigade at Sened Station, inflicting about 100 casualties and taking almost 100 prisoners, for the loss of two American tanks.

A battery of 65/17 guns of the *'La Spezia'* Division's 80th Artillery Regiment in Tunisia, early 1943, being towed by Guzzi Trialce motorcycles. (Enrico Finazzer)

Generaloberst **von Arnim and General Messe, 1943.**

Germans fire an 88 mm gun in Tunisia, 1943.

On 31 January the Americans assaulted Maknassy and ran into determined resistance by *'Centauro'*. The following day American forces succeeded in capturing Sened Station from the Italians. On 2 February command of the *Deutsch-Italienische Panzerarmee*, or *Armata Corazzata Italo-Tedesca*, was assumed by General Giovanni Messe, replacing Rommel, and on 5 February the Italo-German forces became redesignated as the 1ª Armata Italiana (Italian 1st Army). On 10 March *Generaloberst* Hans-Jürgen von Arnim took command of the *Panzerarmee*, while Rommel took command of the *Heeresgruppe Afrika*. Italian 1st Army consisted of three corps which included the Italian *'Trieste'*, *'Pistoia'*, *'La Spezia'* and *'Giovani Fascisti'* divisions, and the German *90.leichte*, *164 leichte* and *15.Panzer-Division*.

The German 5th Army consisted of the newly arrived *334.Infanterie-Division*, the *10.Panzer-Division*, the *21.Panzer-Division* and assorted other smaller units, as well as the Italian *'Superga'* infantry division. By this time, for the first time in North Africa, German troops outnumbered the Italians, 74,000 to 26,000.

A Breda Model 35 20mm antiaircraft gun position. All of the crew are wearing the tropical pith helmet favored by many Italians, especially artillery crews and *Bersaglieri*, in the desert; two of the crew have sand goggles on their helmets. (Massimiliano Afiero)

Tiger tank in a Tunisian village, 1943.

The change in designation was accompanied by command changes as well and on 12 February the *Panzerarmee* command was assumed by General Giovanni Messe. Also on 12 February 1943, two years to the day after Rommel had first arrived in North Africa, the last Italo-German rearguard elements from Libya crossed the border into Tunisia and on 15 February the Mareth line was reached. This ended 2,100 kilometer

(1,300 mile) retreat from El Alamein to Tunisia, plodding along at about 20 kilometers (12 miles) per day for 102 days, of the battered but still dangerous Italian and German forces.

A 47/32 antitank gun well camouflaged in a stand of cacti in Tunisia, 1943. Although obsolete throughout the desert campaign, the Italians continued to use this gun to good effect. (USSME)

Panzer III medium tanks at Kasserine Pass, Tunisia.

Battle of Kasserine

On 13 February the ever-dynamic Rommel assembled his forces for a proposed raid on Gafsa. The attack was to consist of *15.Panzer* with 53 panzers and *'Centauro'* with 23 M14s from El Guettar. *'Centauro'* consisted of the 5th Bersaglieri Regiment (three battalions), two artillery battalions from the 131st Artillery Regiment, one tank battalion and one semovente group. On 14 February the battle of Kasserine Pass began. Coordination between German 5th Army and the Italian 1st Army was not good because of the differing views of their commanders, General Hans-Jürgen von Arnim and General Giovanni Messe. On 19 February *'Centauro'* (one tank battalion and part of 5th Bersaglieri Regiment) was brought up to reinforce *15.Panzer* at Kasserine Pass. The next day, the German assault group resumed its attack against Kasserine Pass; *'Centauro's* tanks were held in reserve to exploit a possible breakthrough. One battalion of *Bersaglieri* on the right flank took Djebel Semmama after a bloody fight.

A group of *Panzer III* medium tanks at Kasserine Pass, Tunisia, February 1943.

Italian semoventes in action, Tunisia 1943.

The Italian action was instrumental in breaking through US positions; *'Centauro'* advanced five miles towards Tebessa, encountering no enemy forces. On 21 February, *15.Panzer* and *'Centauro'* moved from Kasserine Pass to seize Djebel el Hamra, came up against US resistance and failed to reach Djebel el Hamra, and on 22 February, 5th Bersaglieri Regiment was holding a line against strong US counterattacks from Djebel el Hamra. *15.Panzer* and the DLIV self-propelled gruppo launched a counterattack, temporarily relieving pressure on the *Bersaglieri*, but were later counterattacked by US forces which drove the bersaglieri back to Kasserine. On 22 February the attack stalled with not unfavorable results for the

Italo-German forces. About 180 American tanks had been destroyed, along with 210 guns, 200 half-tracks and 510 other vehicles. On 23 February, the remnants of *'Centauro'* pulled back to El Ank and Bir Marabot in the Gafsa area.

A patrol of SPA-Viberti mod. 42 Saharianas in Tunisia in March 1943. The Sahariana was purpose-built for desert operations and was based on the AB41 armored car chassis. The vehicle in the foreground is armed with a 20mm Breda cannon, while the second vehicle mounts a 47/32 antitank gun. (USSME)

Operation 'Capri'

On 6 March following meetings between Rommel and Messe, the Italian 1st Army launched a spoiling attack designated Operation *'Capri'*, designed to take Medenine. The forces consisted largely of German units (elements of the three German panzer divisions, two reconnaissance battalions, five infantry battalions, a parachute battalion and seven field artillery batteries); the Italians contributed the *'La Spezia'* and *'Trieste'* battle groups with two

Italian Tanks during the Battle of Médenine, March 1943.

battalions each, plus assorted miscellaneous units. However, Montgomery had been forewarned by ULTRA intercepts of the impending attack and was therefore prepared for it; after a rather brief encounter the Axis forces abandoned the attack in the evening of the following day, losing about 40 tanks against a loss of only six British tanks and a number of other vehicles and guns. On 17 March General George S. Patton launched the derisively named Operation *'Wop'* to capture Gafsa. The attack consisted of 90,000 men against a mixed Italo-German force of 7,100. *'Centauro'*, acting as a mobile rearguard had 30 M14 tanks, and *10.Panzer-Division* with 50 panzers running, conducted a fighting withdrawal to better positions at El Guettar. At Uadi Mejirda, the I Battalion of *'Trieste'* and II Gruppo of the 21st Artillery, commanded by Captain Mario Politi, with orders to hold out as long as possible, was heavily engaged. It held in the face of repeated attacks until 26 March when Politi was ordered to withdraw.

A Semovente L40 47/32 during an attack, Tunisia 1943.

An M3 Stuart of the 13th Armored Regiment outside of Maknassy, Tunisia 1943. (SC 282399)

On 20 March US forces attacked the *'Imperiali'* Brigade positions at Maknassy. On 21 March what was left of *'Centauro'* fought stubbornly throughout the day and managed to stem the advance of the US 5th Army, which however, on 25 March resumed its advance at El Hamma, towards Gabes. *'Centauro'* held out for about another week, and finally quit the Mareth Line. On 31 March the Italians suffered a serious breakthrough in the center of their line, but the second line strongpoints held firm and artillery stopped the attack with heavy losses to the Americans. The remnants of *'Centauro'* were reduced to a raggruppamento strength with 18 tanks and two SP guns of the XVI Battalion and 31st Regiment (an additional 31 tanks and three SP guns were in the regimental repair depot at Rennouch) that continued fighting at El Guettar alongside *10.Panzer-Division*.

Operation 'Pugilist' (20 March - 22 March 1943)

In the 1930s the French had fortified a line that ran roughly from Gabes on the coast inland to Medenine; the line followed the course of the Wadi Zigzaou, a natural antitank ditch between 60 and 200 feet wide and 20 feet deep and was designed to defend against Italian forces that were stationed in Libya, but in 1940 when the armistice was signed between France and Italy, the fortifications were abandoned by the French. The line took its name from Mareth, which was close to the coast, southeast of Gabes. Italo-German deployments along the line consisted from the sea to the Matmata Hills, of the 136th *'Giovani Fascisti'* division, the 101st *'Trieste'* motorized division, the German *90.leichte-Division*, the 80th *'La Spezia'* infantry (airtransportable) division, the 16th *'Pistoia'* infantry division and the German *164.leichte-Afrika Division*. Also in the Tebaga Gap area, was the *Raggruppamento Sahariano* under General Alberto Mannerini, consisting of one border guard regiment plus another border guard battalion, two machine gun battalions, seven Saharan companies, a squadron group from the *'Lancieri di Novara'* regiment, an artillery group and a mixed engineer battalion. Mobile forces to the rear of the front-line units were the German *15.Panzer* and *21.Panzer* divisions, and the 131st *'Centauro'* armored division; *'Centauro'*, however, had only 38 tanks and six self-propelled guns at its disposal. After initial moves and preparations that were carried out beginning

A *'Giovani Fascisti'* **Mortar, Tunisia 1943.**

as early as 11 March, on 20 March Eighth Army launched Operation *'Pugilist'* against the Mareth Line. The attack began with an intense artillery barrage in the coastal sector held by the Italian infantry divisions, and was followed by a rather weak infantry assault against the Italo-German positions. Apparently, Montgomery, flushed with his continuous string of victories since El Alamein, was overconfident and believed that the forces opposing him would be easy game.

A Giovane Fascista with a Fiat Model 1935 machine gun, date unknown, but likely in Tunisia. (Bruno Benvenuti)

German soldiers fire a 150mm cannon in Tunisia.

However, when the attack was launched, things did not go well for the British. In the northern section of the line, the British 50th and 51st infantry divisions attacked the positions of the *'Giovani Fascisti'* and the *'Trieste'* divisions and made it across the main defensive line at Wadi Zigzaou in the face of spirited Italian resistance, especially by the *'Giovani Fascisti'*. Durham Light Infantry managed to seize Oerzi and Ksiba Ouest by the middle of the night, but the Valentine tanks of the 50th Royal Tank Regiment were unable to get more than a few tanks across Wadi Zigzaou to support the infantry. The next day, 21 March both 50th and 51st divisions, having suffered heavy casualties, were pushed back to the edge of Wadi Zigzaou and withdrew, and on 22 March Montgomery had to acknowledge that the attack had to be called off; his misplaced overconfidence and essentially sloppy planning resulted in an embarrassing failure for Eighth Army.

An M14/41 entering the outskirts of a Tunisian village in 1943. The sign on the side of the road indicates distances to Ste. Marie du Zit, Bou-Ficha and Zriba, all locations roughly 50 to 60 kilometers (31 to 37 miles) south of Tunis. Some attempt at providing camouflage has been made by placing branches on the turret. (USSME)

German Panzer III, Tunisia 1943.

Meanwhile, on 19 March General Freyberg's New Zealand Corps had made it through a gap in the Matmata Hills and by 21 March had reached the Tebaga Gap. However, Freyberg's advance had been detected by General Mannerini, who deployed his Saharan Group, numbering about 2,500 assorted troops to defend the Tebaga Gap. Messe then ordered the German *164.leichte-Division* to pull out of its Mareth Line position and move to support Mannerini, and also redeployed *21.Panzer-Division* to meet the New Zealand threat. The New Zealanders, supported by 8th Armoured Brigade, managed to force a gap during the early morning hours of 22 March but as daylight dawned, the Italians, now reinforced by the German forces that Messe had juggled to send to their aid, blocked any further progress at making it through the Tebaga Gap.

A battery of M41 SP guns on the march in Tunisia in 1943. The rearmost vehicle displays the name 'Colubrina' on the rear plate, indicating that it belongs to the 2nd Battery of the DLIX Gruppo of the *Centauro* armored division. (USSME)

Italian soldiers on a defensive position, Tunisia 1943.

On 24 March General von Arnim, who had replaced Rommel, ordered that the Mareth Line be evacuated beginning the next day, 25 March. Messe's Italian divisions were to pull back to the Wadi Akarit line, where they would make yet another stand against the rather ponderous and at times stumbling, but ever implacable advance of the Eighth Army. While the units were pulling out of the Mareth positions, on 26 March Montgomery launched Operation '*Supercharge II*' which was aimed at engaging the German armor and eventually seizing El Hamma behind the Mareth Line. Messe continued to move the

Italian infantry to the Wadi Akarit line, and by 29 March what was left of the German panzers likewise pulled back to Wadi Akarit which the British reached the next day. As soon as the Italian divisions had reached the Akarit positions they began to dig in and improve their defensive positions.

A 47/32 SP gun in an overwatch position in Tunisia, 1943. The small size of this vehicle made it relatively easy to camouflage, as has been done on this vehicle by using readily available vegetation. (USSME)

Desert patrol vehicle of the Auto-Saharan Company, an Italian Camionetta Desertica AS 42 Sahariana, Tunisia 1943.

The Wadi Akarit line was shorter than the Mareth Line had been, and like it, was anchored on the coast. Despite the relatively favorable defensive terrain, the Italian and German divisions had suffered from attrition during the fighting along the Mareth Line and the Tebaga Gap and were therefore somewhat weaker in terms of manning. From the sea inland, the deployment consisted of *90.leichte-Division* and the *'Giovani Fascisti'*, with *'Pistoia'*, *'La Spezia'* and *'Trieste'* divisions in the center, and *164.leichte-Division* and Mannerini's Saharan Group holding the right of the line. These forces were backed by *15.Panzer-*

Division as a mobile counterattack force, while *10.Panzer*, *21.Panzer* and *'Centauro'* were to the northwest, facing the Americans near El Guettar. Prospects were not bright for the Italo-German forces. On 6 April, Eighth Army attacked the Akarit positions; the main attack, made by British 50th and 51st infantry divisions and by 4th Indian Division was directed against the Italian infantry divisions (*'Pistoia'*, *'La Spezia'* and *'Trieste'*) in the center of the line. Although the Italians fought stubbornly and fiercely, *'Trieste'* was eventually overwhelmed by the sheer numbers of the attacking infantry.

A column of 47/32 SP guns moving in Tunisia in 1943. Five battalions of these guns were deployed to Tunisia. (USSME)

A German Tiger tank in action, Tunisia 1943.

By that evening, with the units low on ammunition, Messe gave the order to pull back some 280 kilometers (about 175 miles) to Enfidaville. The mobile units (essentially the German units) began to pull back using their organic transport, while the Italian units, as usual lacking transport assets, once again began their march on foot. It is no wonder that of the 7,000 Axis troops who were

The Axis Forces

Tunisia, 1943. An Italian medic from the *La Spezia* Division treats the hand of a wounded German NCO.

Italian Breda 35 20 mm anti aircraft gun, Tunisia 1943.

***Folgore* Parachute soldiers during the Battle of Takrouna.**

captured, the bulk were Italian; they could not pull back fast enough on foot to outrun the pursuing British and neither did they have the time, the ammunition, or any easily defensible terrain that would allow them to even attempt to make another stand on their own. Averaging about 25 miles per day, shredded remnants of the Italian and German forces almost miraculously managed to maintain some semblance of unit cohesion and reached Enfidaville by 12 and 13 April. Both the German and Italian forces were severely depleted; the worst of the lot was probably the '*La Spezia*' division, which was down to less than two companies. Nonetheless, from 13 to 30 April the Italians fended off a series of attacks by British forces. The most noteworthy of these actions for the Italians was the defense of Takrouna by '*Trieste*'; that division held the center of the Axis line, and defending Takrouna which was deemed to be a key point of the defensive system, was the I Battalion of the 66th Regiment and an attached German platoon under the command of the overworked Captain Politi. Politi's father had somewhat prophetically bestowed the middle name of Leonida, the Greek hero of the defense of Thermopylae, upon Mario, who would more than live up to the name in the days to come. Between 16 and 18 April the British pounded Takrouna, which consisted of a small village atop a modest limestone crop hill feature, with artillery. To the left of Takrouna, at Dj Bir, was a company of the German 47th Regiment. Politi had organized a 360-degree defense and had planned to lay mines along the entire perimeter, but the attack prevented that initiative.

A column of M14/41 italian tanks on the march in Tunisia in 1943.

An Italian antitank position of the *'Folgore'*, Tunisia 1943.

At dawn on 20 April, enemy infantry supported by tanks began to attack. The German positions at Dj Bir were overcome after putting up fierce resistance. New Zealand Maori infantry infiltrated the southern slopes of the hill and attempted to climb from the southwest, but were stopped by fire from the 4th Company, which took some prisoners; the Italian chaplain later counted 150 enemy dead. The Maoris continued to attack, however, and overwhelmed the positions held by the 2nd Company; this enabled the Maoris to break into the houses in the town. Politi then led the headquarters platoon in a counterattack to relieve pressure on the 1st Company. The battalion infirmary was about to be overrun, but the New Zealanders were driven off at the last moment by a number of hand grenades thrown by the chaplain, Don Giuseppe Maccariello. As the situation grew more serious, *'Trieste'* sent two companies of *'Folgore'* paratroopers and a company of *'Granatieri'* to reinforce the position. The *'Folgore'* troopers, in house-to-house fighting, were able to flush the Maoris out of the buildings in Takrouna, and by the night of 20 April Politi had managed to stabilize the situation. On 21 April the positions were once again taken under heavy artillery fire, and fresh enemy troops were thrown into the fray, and the Italian positions began to be overwhelmed. At 1445, Politi sent the following message to *'Trento'* headquarters: *'Situation extremely critical, desperate stop. We have fired our last cartridges stop. Losses are very heavy stop. The enemy has occupied almost all of our positions stop. Very many enemy infantry which continues to increase stop. They have a lot of tanks down below stop. Situation desperate stop. Hurry up, hurry up, Politi.'*

General Messe (on the left), with other Italian officers, on the Tunisian front, 1943.

German prisoners wait in a roadside ditch after a British counter-attack, April 1943.

An attempt to send the 103rd Arditi Company as a relief force failed, and at 1705, *'Trieste'* received a message that the radio center was under attack; this was followed by silence. By the night of 21 April the *'Trieste'* battalion's position at Takrouna had fallen. Of the initial 560 men, subsequently reinforced by a further 300, only about 50 managed to escape unharmed. The action earned Politi his third Silver Medal, as well as a battlefield promotion to major. On 25 April (Easter Sunday) the 6th New Zealand Brigade attacked the sector held by the *'Giovani Fascisti'*, particularly Point 141; the Italians suffered 156 killed, wounded and missing, but counted about 150 dead enemy bodies in front of their positions. Point 141 changed hands several times afterwards but was finally taken definitively by the 'Giovani Fasciti's 3rd Company, which was reduced to only 20 men at the end of the fighting. Between 9 and 13 May during the so-called Second Battle of Enfidaville, Point 141 continued to be held by the *'Giovani Fascisti'*; on 10 May *90.leichte-Division* surrendered, but the *'Giovani Fascisti'* continued to hold out until the announcement of surrender on 13 May.

The last relatively noteworthy success scored by Italian armor in North Africa was on 25 April at Gebel bou Kurnine, when the recently arrived DLIX self-propelled gun group, also known as *Gruppo Piscicelli*, with 12 SP guns and 12 M14/41 tanks of the 'Centauro's XIV Battalion, engaged attacking British tanks for two hours and drove them off, knocking out about 28. Parenthetically, Piscicelli, who had been dubbed by his men as the *'Duca della Scala'* during Operation *'Crusader'*, had left Libya and returned to Italy in early 1942 but in April 1943 was requested by Messe to return to North Africa because of his expertise in artillery employment. On 26 April 'Centauro's' last ten M14s were integrated into *10.Panzer* and *'Centauro'* was officially disbanded.

On 6 May five self-propelled guns from *Gruppo Piscicelli* ambushed the extreme left flank of an Allied armored column, but Piscicelli's own vehicle was hit, seriously wounding him. The surviving SP guns held off the attacking tanks for a few hours, protecting the German artillery at Maharine, at the request of *15.Panzer-Division*. The group then managed to reach the Mateur-Tunis road junction. On 8 May the last engagement by the self-propelled guns took place on the road that led to Porto Farina by a group consisting of four SP guns and the lone tank of Second Lieutenant Orlando of XV Battalion, a few panzers and an 88mm gun battery. Two of the SP guns were hit and a few German tanks were set on fire. A pair of semoventi still continued to fight, firing their last remaining rounds and knocking out an American tank.

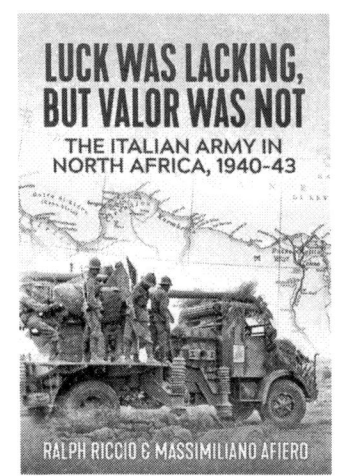

On 9 May the German 5th Army surrendered to US II Corps, while the Italian 1st Army continued to resist until 13 May when Messe surrendered, definitively ending the Axis presence in North Africa. The figures for losses on both sides vary somewhat depending on the source consulted. For the period of the Tunisian campaign on the Axis side, the Italians lost some 3,700 men killed, while the Germans lost about 8,500 killed, and another 40,000-50,000 Italian and German soldiers were wounded. About 90,000 Italians were taken prisoner along with about 102,000 Germans. On the opposing side, the British and Commonwealth forces suffered about 6,200 killed, 21,500 wounded and 10,500 missing. The Free French also lost about 2,150 killed and 10,250 wounded. The Americans, latecomers to the fighting, incurred about 2,700 killed, 9,000 wounded and 6,500 missing.

Bibliography
Massimiliano Afiero & Ralph Riccio, "*Luck was lacking, but Valor was not, the Italian Army in North Africa, 1940-1943*", Helion & Company Limited

The SS-Division Wiking towards the Caucasus, Summer 1942

by Massimiliano Afiero

A *Wiking*'s *PzKpfw.III* on the march, 1942.

Grenadiers and tanks of the *Wiking*, 1942.

The countryside changed quickly, it was no longer the Ukraine, but a strange world where the inhabitants had dark hair and laughed heartily. The villages were pleasant and full of flowers, the fields were red and yellow: tomatoes and corn. The attack by the German forces coincided with the harvest season for the fruit. Tanks and trucks moved through pear and apple trees. The fruits were enormous, full of juice and sun. The soldiers filled their bellies until they gorged themselves. For Steiner, however, this was not a pleasure trip; to reach the Kuban River as quickly as possible had become almost an obsession for him. To that end, he kept pushing his battalions forward, ordering them to keep strictly to the march tables. *Panzers* and *Stukas* perfected new attack techniques which destroyed Soviet defensive positions one after another. However, according to aerial reconnaissance reports, the *Wiking* units were advancing in the midst of a large concentration of retreating enemy troops. But by now it was already too late to reach the Kuban before the Soviets. Following a long night march between 28 and 29 July, the *Wiking Panzergruppe*, continuing to consist of Mühlenkamp's panzers and Dieckmann's grenadiers, captured the position at Metchetinskaja. The advance then continued on to the south-east, as far as Jegorlykskaja, another position that was defended doggedly by Soviet units. *Kampfgruppe von Scholz* also joined in under the command of the commander of the *Nordland* Regiment, *SS-Obf.* Fritz von Scholz, while the *Westland* was still on the march to join up with the rest of the division. Mühlenkamp's panzers proceeded towards Ssred-Jergolyk, where they were subjected to a counterattack mounted by the Soviets during the night of 31 July and 1 August, which was fended off by the SS units with heavy enemy losses. The next objective was Bjelaja-Glina (Bjelajgalina), an important road and rail hub along the Tichorez-Ssalk railway line, which had to be captured.

Wiking's soldiers in the southern sector of Bjelaja-Glina (*Charles Trang Collection*).

SS-Stubaf. Karl Schlamelcher.

The mission was given to *Kampfgruppe Gille*, which reached the outskirts of the city with its guns on the afternoon of August 1. At the same time, the panzers circled the position from the west, operating in coordination with Dieckmann's battalion coming from the south-west, to cut off the enemy's retreat while the other two battalions of the *Germania* led by *SS-Staf.* Wagner made a frontal attack. Soviet resistance was overcome and the German soldiers were welcomed warmly by the civilian population who offered, according to their custom, bread and salt. During these clashes, *SS-Stubaf.* Karl Schlamelcher, commander of *III./SS-Art.Rgt.5*, suffered a grievous head wound.

The Kuban front

On August 4, 1942, German forces reached the banks of the Kuban. This was not only a river, but many swift water courses that fell from the Caucasus mountains, which formed a web with each other and which made crossing impossible. The Germans had not yet been able to find an intact bridge. *SS-Gruf.* Steiner had received his orders. He was to cross the river at two points. For one objective, he was to take the city of Kropotkin, twenty-five kilometers from the spearhead of the division, which with a wide encircling movement had already been marching to the west for several days. The other objective was to cross the Kuban further to the east, at Grigori-Politskaja.

A column of *Wiking* panzers on the Kuban front (*Pierre Tiquet Collection*).

A *Marder II* of *SS-Pz.Jg.Abt. 'Wiking'* (NA).

The commander, assisted by his chief of staff, *SS-Stubaf.* Reichel, went to work and divided his forces into two *Kampfgruppen*, with units from *Germania* and *Nordland*, both reinforced with panzers from *SS-Stubaf.* Mühlenkamp. Soon after, the two combat groups were given their orders: the first group, led by *SS-Staf.* Jürgen Wagner, with elements of *Germania*, was to push to the south-east, with the mission of attacking Grigori-Politskaja. The second group, led by *SS-Obf.* Von Scholz, with elements of the *Nordland* regiment, was to push to the south-west to prepare to take the village of Kropotkin, seize the bridge over the Kuban, and cross the river. After that, both of the *Wiking* division's *Kampfgruppen* were to continue on to the Asian territories of the Caucasus. At Grigori-Politskaja the Soviet forces had dug themselves in and were in fact getting ready to mount a counter-attack. Mühlenkamp's panzers attached to *Kampfgruppe Wagner* had been ordered to invest the enemy positions, wipe them out and reach the river.

A *Wiking* infantry unit on the march on the Kuban front, Summer 1942 (NARA).

***SS-Hstuf*. Hans Dorr (left) with his grenadiers (NARA)**

The grenadiers of Dieckmann's assault battalion marched behind the panzers, advancing rapidly without worrying to clear the area. That task was left to the other companies of the *Germania*. In front of them, the Soviets fought like lions, defending every foot of ground with fierce determination. Leading the battalion was the 1st Company under *SS-Hstuf*. Hans Dorr. His unit consisted of volunteers from Denmark, Norway, Holland and Flanders. Along with their comrades from Dieckmann's battalion, Dorr's men passed through Grigori-Politskaja, then continued on quickly towards the river, passing through the forests. The engineers under *SS-Stubaf*. Schäfer were the first to reach the Kuban, with rubber rafts and wooden boats. During the night between August 4-5, the boats were pushed into the river's raging waters. Crowded up against each other, the men of the assault group of Dorr's company tried to see the enemy shore. Every once in a while flares went off and everyone lowered their heads as soon as the first machine gun burst began. Geysers of water spouted from the explosions.

SS-Stubaf. **August Dieckmann (left) while crossing the Kuban, August 1942 (NARA).**

Wiking **soldiers crossing the Kuban.**

Dorr directed his men onto a small island right in the middle of the river, hiding them in the vegetation. At dawn on August 5, they moved out from that position to attack the western bank of the river, defended by Soviet units. All of the boats seemed to move out of their hiding places at the same time. Soon after, the leading elements of the company took up positions on the other bank. A machine gun was quickly emplaced to respond to enemy fire. Within a short time, Dieckmann's entire battalion had crossed the Kuban under the fire of Soviet guns and mortars. But by then it was too late. The Germanic volunteers were on the western bank of the river and would not be leaving it. On the eastern shore, some *Wiking* panzers fired without letup to cover the crossing of the grenadiers. By then *SS-Hstuf.* Dorr was in control of the Grigori-Politskaja bridgehead on the other side of the

Kuban. Throughout that first night the Soviets attempted to throw the SS grenadiers back across the river, continually attacking the German bridgehead. Furious close-quarter fighting broke out, the bloodiest the *Wiking* had experienced since the beginning of the campaign. During that same night another company of the *Germania* was able to cross the river, reinforcing the bridgehead. Hans Dorr moved from position to position to check on his men. Everything seemed as it should be, the machine gunners were in place and the grenadiers waited for the next Soviet counter-attack with apparent calm.

Wiking **soldiers in combat in the Kuban sector, August 1942 (*Charles Trang Collection*).**

A *Wiking* **soldier during an attack, August 1942.**

The night of August 5/6, was even rougher. Soviet attacks continued without letup beginning at two in the morning. At dawn, Dorr personally led a counter-attack that managed to regain some ground. Around noon new reinforcements arrived which made it possible to expand the bridgehead and to capture the local church, which provided an excellent observation point. Once the bridgehead had been solidly reinforced, *SS-Staf.* Wagner crossed the river with the other two battalions of *Germania*, the II. under Jörchel and the III. under Schönfelder. The engineers of the divisional engineer battalion also attacked. It was now necessary to build a temporary bridge as soon as possible, under enemy fire, to enable the other units of the division to cross. All of *Kampfgruppe Wagner* thus was able to cross the river.

A machine gunner and his assistant (ammunition carrier) engaged in combat with their *MG-34*.

The battle for Kropotkin

While *Kampfgruppe Wagner* attacked towards Grigori-Politskaja, *Kampfgruppe von Scholz* had been assigned the mission to capture, on the other side of Kropotkin, the only bridge capable of supporting the weight of the panzers. *Nordland*'s Scandinavian and German volunteers were supported by the armoured battalion's 1st Company, commanded by *SS-Ostuf.* Schnabel. The commander himself, Mühlenhamp, had decided to participate in this operation of vital importance. On August 5, *SS-Ostuf.* Klapdor's platoon was at the head of the column marching towards Kropotkin. His panzers forged ahead at full speed, with the infantry's combat vehicles following closely behind as if glued to them, part of the infernal rhythm of the operation. As they moved towards battle, the SS soldiers seated in their vehicles continued to eat fruit that they had gathered at the previous stop. When they were close

Wiking Pz.Kpfw.II on the march, along with other vehicles.

to the city without encountering any resistance along the way, the SS vehicles began to slow down. The four tanks of Klapdor's platoon went slowly down the sloping road that led into the city and towards the river. The panzers advanced slowly along the tortuous route, completely in the open, ready to halt and fire at any moment.

Wiking **panzers on the march towards Kropotkin, August 1942.**

Panzers on the march towards Kropotkin. *SS-Ustuf*. Martin's tank can be seen in the distance, hit by enemy fire and in flames.

When he reached the centre of Kropotkin, Klapdor stuck his head out of the turret, but there was no one there, the city appeared completely deserted, with not a soldier or a civilian to be seen. There were no obstacles in the streets. There was deathly silence under the scorching August sun. Klapdor quickly found the road that led to the bridge. Klapdor's tanks were then overtaken by the engineer platoon led by *SS-Ustuf*. Martin. Motorcycles and armoured cars then took the lead of the column and guided the entire *1.Kompanie* to the bridge and

SS-Stubaf. **Mühlenhamp** (*Pierre Tiquet Collection*).

A *Wiking* SdKfz.222 with his 20mm gun.

the river. The *Nordland* grenadiers followed on both sides of the road, weapons in hand, ready to react to any appearance by the enemy. The city continued to remain quiet, behind its closed shutters. *SS-Staf.* von Scholz passed to the head of the column in an armoured car, raising a cloud of dust. Old Fritz wanted to be the first to reach the Kuban: *"..Forward, faster!"* he yelled at his men! *SS-Ostuf.* Schnabel, commander of the 1st Tank Company, then ordered Klapdor to close the column with his platoon. Then he drove on to reach the leading panzer. *SS-Stubaf.* Mühlenhamp was with him in the column, in his command tank, between the two leading platoons. The *Wiking* armoured vehicles moved along a raised road just in front of a bend in the river. Only a few trees provided cover from enemy observation. The Soviets were nowhere to be seen and the panzers, escorted by the *Nordland* grenadiers, continued to march on towards the bridge over the Kuban. In the lead, with Old Fritz, were the motorcyclists, the armoured cars and the *PzKpfw.II* led by Sepp Martin. The silence continued to be oppressive. All of a sudden there was a loud explosion and a cloud of smoke could be seen in the distance, followed by the sinister noise of the bridge collapsing into the riverbed; the Soviets had set off the charges under the bridge, the only crossing over the Kuban in that area. Soon after there were two more explosions, this time coming from the railway line. Two convoys of tank cars, full of gasoline and motor oil, exploded violently. An immense cloud of black smoke obscured the sky over Kropotkin. As though those explosions had been signals, the Soviets began to fire on the German column, at first with automatic weapons and then with mortars and artillery. Some well-camouflaged enemy anti-tank guns had remained on the eastern bank and immediately opened fire on the *Wiking* tanks. The panzers quickly returned fire while the soldiers took cover. *SS-Staf.* von Scholz was furious; he would not be able to cross the river, at least for the time being. He had no choice but to defend the city.

A *Wiking* PzKpfw.III during the fighting in the Kuban (*Giorgio Bussano Collection*).

SS-Staf. **Fritz von Scholz.**

His soldiers headed for the city, entered the houses and took prisoners. Immobilized near the river on the outskirts of Kropotkin, two or three tanks from the lead platoon, under enemy fire, tried to take cover to the left of the road in a defilade position. Right in front of the destroyed bridge an isolated panzer had begun to fire against the anti-tank guns that the Soviets had emplaced on the opposite bank. Exposed as it was to enemy fire, it was soon hit by a Soviet anti-tank gun; smoke began to billow from the vents, it was dead in its tracks, the engine was about to catch fire. The crew was stoic and continued to fire against the Soviet positions. The other tanks that were on the road had spotted the danger coming from their right, but the thick vegetation prevented them from identifying the enemy locations. The situation of *SS-Ostuf.* Schnabel's *1.Kompanie* continued to become increasingly critical, due partly to a break in radio communications. *SS-Ostuf.* Klapdor, who was at the tail end of the column, got out of his tank to take stock of the situation. Walking along the left side of the road, he tried to reach Mühlenhamp's tank. Taken under fire by an enemy machine gun, the *SS-Ostuf.* jumped into a ditch beside the road and from there reached the commander: *"...What do you want?"* asked Mühlenhamp. *"Knock out those damned anti-tank guns"* repled Klapdor. *"And how am I supposed to do that?"* Mühlenhamp asked again.

Panzer of the 1.Kp./SS-Pz.Abt.5 on the march along the railway line (Charles Trang).

SS-Ostuf. Ewald Klapdor.

Then Klapdor laid out his plan:*"...Going along the right side of the road, protected by the trees, it would be possible to reach the river and knock them out"*. Mühlenhamp reflected on it for a moment. It was a dangerous move, but it was the only way possible to get out of that difficult situation. Klapdor, being at the end of the column, could maneuver more easily. *"Go ahead then"* ordered Mühlenhamp. Klapdor's panzers advanced as planned and once they had reached the vicinity of the river began to destroy the enemy anti-tank guns one by one. Anything that moved along the southern bank was hit by fire from the tanks, forcing the enemy to stay under cover and preventing him from returning fire. *SS-Staf.* von Scholz then reached Mühlenhamp to assess the situation. The city of Kropotkin was in their hands but the main objective, to cross the river, had escaped them. The only thing that was left of the bridge were a few shaky columns. Numerous Soviet deserters swam across the river and were quickly taken to the *Kampfgruppe* headquarters; the provided important information concerning the location and strength of Soviet forces in the area.

Wiking **Panzers crossing the railway line near Kropotkin, August 1942.**

SS-Oberführer **Jürgen Wagner.**

The Scandinavian and German volunteers of *Nordland* were then ordered to cross the river on rafts and boats, under enemy fire.

Continued fighting at Grigori-Politskaja

In the Grigori-Politskaja sector, the *Kampfgruppe Wagner* grenadiers continued to expand their bridgehead. The Soviets counter-attacked until dawn on August 6, employing all of their artillery. Once again the German felt the overwhelming power of Soviet artillery which was capable of concentrating dozens and dozens of pieces in some sectors. They tried to create a veritable wall of fire while giving their infantry time to regroup and to attack and reduce the bridgehead. On the western bank of the Kuban, the German forces held on to a narrow strip of ground. The Soviet guns targeted the *Wiking* artillery batteries, which were forced to continually shift position. As soon as they occupied a new position, enemy shells began to fall, causing injuries among the crews. How could their fire be so accurate? There surely had to be a Soviet artillery observer in the area who was providing precise reporting. *SS-Staf.* Wagner then sent out patrols to Grigori-Politskaja. In order to locate the observers the elevated vantage points were plotted; the first of these were church steeples of the old churches. Two Soviet officers were discovered in one of them.

Wiking **soldiers crossing the Kuban near Grigori-Politskaja, August 1944 (NARA).**

Wiking **soldiers and a 50mm anti-tank gun crossing the Kuban, August 1955 (NARA).**

The SS soldiers tried to capture them, but the chose to die fighting rather than surrendering. From that time on, the Soviet artillery fire began to be less accurate. On August 7, the engineers were able to complete a crossing for the panzers across the river; the *Wiking* tanks quickly went on the attack against the enemy artillery batteries, which were already in a state of panic following an attack by *Stukas*. In the midst of those explosions, the Soviet guns were reduced to silence one after another. Devastated by bombs from the *Stukas* and shells from the panzers, the Soviet gunners suffered horrific losses. A few undamaged guns fell into the hands of the grenadiers from *Germania* who had been advancing behind the panzers. At that point, nothing could threaten the bridgehead. The remaining Soviet forces were forced to withdraw across the Laba River. Once the Kuban had been crossed, the next objective was the city of Maikop, one of the capitals of the Soviet oil empire.

From the left, *SS-Ustuf.* Werner Hein, *SS-Ostuf.* Willi Klose and *SS-Stubaf.* August Dieckmann at the Grigori-Politskaja bridgehead, August 1942 (NARA).

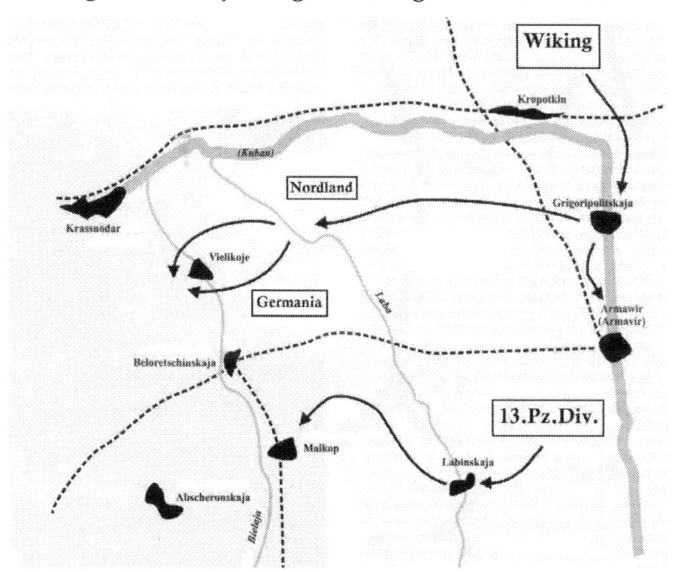

The areas involved in the early August fighting.

The march resumes

The march of the *Wiking* units resumed from the bridgehead established by the *Germania* on the Kuban River. The division was split into three combat groups, led by von Scholz, Gille and Wagner. This time, *Nordland* was to take the lead, in accordance with the old warrior's code of alternating the lead. Then the column was to split again to mount attacks against two locations: *Kampfgruppe von Scholz* was to push to Temirgojewskaja, while *Kampfgruppe Wagner* was to advance towards Petropawloskaja. As always, it was necessary to capture intact as many bridges as possible. On the other side, the Soviets had gathered all of their reserves, including many sailors of the Black Sea Fleet who had left their ships to fight as infantry, in an attempt to stall the German advance on Maikop. This motley force occupied an improvised defensive line whose only solid features were the desperate courage and spirit of sacrifice of the defenders.

A column of Wiking panzers on the march, August 1942.

Wiking soldiers on the march, August 1942.

On their side, the Germans fielded elite troops: *SS-Staf.* von Scholz sent his scouts forward to "test" the enemy forces and to gather intelligence. Everything pointed to a Soviet willingness to fight to the bitter end, and so Old Fritz decided to send his units into the attack that same night, to prevent the enemy from reinforcing any further. German soldiers and Scandinavian volunteers attacked following the panzers of the armoured battalion. The first objective was Temirgojewskaja, which was doggedly defended by Soviet units. Leading the *Nordland* attack, in the wake of the panzers, was the 3rd Company led by *SS-Hstuf.* Friedrich Bluhm. The new line of Soviet resistance was anchored along the Laba River. Towards evening, the German units reached the outskirts of Temirgojewskaja. *SS-Hstuf.* Bluhm quickly issued orders to is platoon leaders: *"..We are in front of the city. We will attack at night, cross the river and establish a bridgehead on the other side of the Laba"*. A few hours later the combat groups began to move silently towards their objectives. The infantry were accompanied by sappers from the engineers who would neutralize the explosive charges and try to capture the bridge intact. The attack began around one in the morning.

A *Wiking* assault group in combat, August 1942 (NARA).

Wiking soldiers with an *MG-34*, August 1942 (NARA).

The Germanic volunteers advanced silently, like ghosts, careful not to lose contact with their comrades in the darkness. They then reached the first houses of the city. Suddenly the point elements thought they could make out figures in the night. Enemies or friends? In doubt, there was a burst of machine gun fire. Other explosions followed. The entire company headed for the bridge, following their captain *"..Forward, forward!"* Bluhm continued to shout. The infantrymen had to cross a road that was being laced by bursts of enemy machine gun fire. Most of the men managed to cross unscathed, only a few were wounded. The river should be in front of the assault troops. A few seconds later, there was a huge detonation. As had happened at Kropotkin, the Soviets had been quicker and the bridge was blown sky-high. The SS troopers were then engaged in clearing the city streets. There was little left of the bridge following the explosion. A few engineers who had managed to cross to the other bank were completely cut off. *SS-Hstuf.* Bluhm sought to provide them supporting fire, but his soldiers were pressed close to the ground by the fire from the Soviet machine guns which fired without letup from the opposite bank. Then the Soviets counter-attacked, using the ruined bridge to cross the river; furious close-quarter fighting ensued, at the end of which the SS soldiers prevailed.

***Wiking* panzers on the move through forests (*Charles Trang Collection*).**

A *Wiking* assault group in combat, August 1942 (NARA).

The fighting became even more intense in the morning, mainly involving the machine gunners, who had engaged in a veritable long-range duel with the Soviet soldiers dug in on the other side of the river. The arrival of some mortar squads enabled the enemy fire positions to be eliminated and soon after *SS-Hstuf.* Bluhm decided that it was the right time to cross over to the other bank. Some of the engineers jumped onto the ruins of the bridge to jury-rig a crossing using wooden planks. The Soviet soldiers made themselves known again, firing on the engineers. The SS mortars and machine guns began firing at a fearful rate, and it was the Soviets who had to bury their heads. The work of the engineers was able to resume, using the bridge abutments that were still intact. In less than an hour a jury-rigged footbridge was built. *SS-Hstuf.* Bluhm threw his men one after another onto the southern bank of the river. A bridgehead had to be established and held at all costs.

Wiking **panzers on the move through villages (*Charles Trang Collection*).**

A *PzKpfw.III Ausf. J* in the Laba sector, August 1942.

The Soviet troops had disappeared into the underbrush and the Germanic volunteers fired in all directions to avoid being surprised. The SS soldiers advanced slowly and cautiously, protected by a hellish fire. Once his men had fanned out for about five hundred meters, he ordered them to stop and to dig into the positions they had reached. It was about nine in the morning when the fighting ceased. The sun was already high in the sky and it was already hot. The platoon leaders were busy setting up a continuous defensive perimeter, ordering their men to: "*Camouflage yourselves well, the Soviets might return*". Trees were thus felled to make fences and bunkers to reinforce the new defensive positions. For their part, the Soviets began to hit the bridgehead with artillery fire, without however being able to dislodge the German units. At Petropawlowskaja as well, the Soviet forces had put up a stiff resistance and had been able to blow the bridge prior to the arrival of the German units.

Panzers from the *Wiking* crossing the Belaja on a pontoon bridge (*Charles Trang Collection*).

SS soldiers engaged in combat, August 1942.

Then another bridge was found in the Tenginskaja area, which was captured on August 8, by *Wiking* armoured units. The engineers were able to repair the bridge so that the division's vehicles could cross it. And thus, *Kampfgruppe von Scholz* as well as the *Kampfgruppe* under *SS-Staf.* Wagner crossed the Laba River at that position on August 9, 1942. The *Wehrmacht* daily report stated that: *"..Army and SS motorized units have crossed the Laba river and are now attacking to the west towards Maikop"*.

In the meantime, the *Wiking* units had resumed their march. The lead had been assumed by *Kampfgruppe Gille*, consisting of grenadiers from *SS-Stubaf.* Dieckmann's assault battalion, by the battalion under *SS-Stubaf.* Polewacz and the *Nordland* regiment and elements of Mühlenhamp's armoured battalion. *SS-Staf.* Wagner with the *Germania* regiment and *SS-Obf.* von Scholz with the *Nordland* regiment followed closely behind. The new direction of march was oriented more to the west, towards Maikop, in an attempt to bag the enemy forces fighting in that sector in a large pocket. Speed and determination were needed to accomplish this new mission.

Wiking soldier armed with an MP-40, engaged in combat, August 1942.

A *Wiking* MG-34 in combat (NARA).

On towards Maikop

The panzers of the *Wiking* continued to advance in the midst of retreating Soviet columns. When the German tanks appeared, the Soviet soldiers dispersed and tried to hide in the sunflower fields that extended on both sides of the roads. Abandoned equipment and vehicles were everywhere, no one had time to stop and collect anyone or anything. The next river that had to be reached was the Belaja; the *Nordland* infantry had climbed aboard the panzers that were driving at full speed through the sunflower fields. Bluhm's company continued in the lead. Vehicles full of SS soldiers followed the panzers that often kicked up clouds of dust. Only the heads of the tank commanders could be seen poking out of their turrets. Some armoured cars of the reconnaissance detachment, accompanied by motorcycles, had joined the column and went forward to scout out suspect villages. There was no time to lose. If the Soviets had any anti-tank guns in this sector, they had to be eliminated and the march continued despite the inevitable losses. Every once in a while the column came to a halt for about ten minutes; the sound of fighting could be heard in the distance. This happened when the lead elements of the recon patrols were engaged in a firefight. The spearhead of the *Wiking* division drew closer to the Belaja River; the ground became increasingly wooded and therefore better suited to ambush by the enemy. The vehicles carrying the SS soldiers halted while the panzers continued to move forward. There were many Soviet units in the area, dug into defensive positions along the banks of the river.

A *Wiking* assault group in combat, August 1942 (NARA).

Bluhm's company was ordered to establish a bridgehead, but first a place to ford had to be found: " ...*We will be supported by the panzers which will remain on this bank. The bank facing us seems to be free of the enemy*". At that point the river was about sixty meters wide, the "enemy" bank was two to three meters high and was very wooded. To the right the ground seemed move level and swampy with scattered woods. *SS-Hstuf.* Bluhm decided to attack in that area and ordered his troops to cross the river. The current was very strong. There was no sign of the enemy, total silence reigned. The first men entered the river; the water reached their knees, then to their waist, then to their chest. The water was very cold. Bluhm's soldiers had to hold each other by the hand to avoid being swept away by the current. Suddenly, one of the panzers on the opposite bank let loose a round. The Soviets returned fire, inflicting the first wounds. It could not be determined where the fire came from. They had to get out of that dangerous situation. The SS troops got closer to the enemy-held bank. As soon as the first men left the river, they quickly emplaced a machine gun to provide covering fire for their comrades. With the arrival of the other assault groups, the bridgehead began to take shape and the men began to fan out, shoulders to the river. At twilight, *SS-Hstuf.* Bluhm decided to enlarge the bridgehead to the right, on more protected ground. The company deployed in a semicircle, anchored on the river. The panzers also managed to slowly wade across the river, as did also the other companies of *Nordland*. **(To be continued)**

Bibliography
Massimiliano Afiero, "*La SS-Division Wiking nel Caucaso 1942-1943*", Ass. Cult. Ritterkreuz
Massimiliano Afiero, "*The SS-Division Wiking in the Caucasus 1942-1943*", MMPbooks
Massimiliano Afiero, "*5.SS-Panzer-Division Wiking volume I, 1941-1943*", Ass. Cult. Ritterkreuz

Printed in Great Britain
by Amazon